THE

Seniority System

IN

Congress

T H E

Seniority System

I N

Congress

Barbara Hinckley

INDIANA UNIVERSITY PRESS

Bloomington / London

Library of Congress catalog card number: 70-138414

ISBN: 253-18025-2

Published in Canada by Fitzhenry & Whiteside Limited,
Don Mills, Ontario

Manufactured in the United States of America

CONTENTS

TABLES

Preface

I APPROACHED THE SENIORITY SYSTEM in early 1967 with the idea that the conventional wisdom on the subject had misread its operation and effects. It appeared that the critics of seniority 1) did not understand the system, 2) might not wish to change it if they did understand it, and, in any case 3) might not be able to change it even if they still wished to. (Changing the seniority system being something on the order of redirecting ocean currents or similar endeavors.) Therefore information on the subject seemed important in refining and redirecting views of congressional operation. Also political scientists had some responsibility in supplying that kind of political information.

Three years later, I am still convinced of the need and "relevance" of that kind of information. But I am more aware that the book only begins to probe the process of congressional leadership selection and I am less optimistic about "redirecting" the conventional wisdom on the subject. (Conventional wisdom is in the same class of durability with the seniority system and the ocean currents.) In the folklore of Congress the seniority system conventionally plays the fiend—whether it wears the Southern or Northern, conservative or liberal garb. It was criticized in the 1850's for giving Senate chairmanships to slave-holding states, in the 1890's for benefiting "Yankee tenacity and longevity," in the 1940's–1960's for its conservative and Southern bias. But by 1970 it was allowing "ultra-liberals" to delay legislation of the Nixon Administration. It was a chief target of reformist concern in the 1940's and is still a chief target today. Against this, one empirical study seems little match for a folklore where, after all, fiends serve important functions.

Nevertheless, the book is offered in the same spirit it was approached and written—as one contribution to the widening area of knowledge about congressional processes and patterns of leadership selection.

Contributing to the final product were a number of individuals who read and criticized this and earlier drafts. To the late Clinton Rossiter, supervisor of the original dissertation, I owe an admiration and gratitude which cannot be repaid. Andrew Hacker, Leroy Rieselbach, and Aaron Wildavsky made important suggestions. Theodore Lowi and Allan Sindler helped shape early thinking on the project. Miriam S. Farley of Indiana University Press supplied penetrating, painstaking (and necessary) editorial revision. And Doris Holden of Amherst, Massachusetts performed the near-herculean labor of intelligent and excellent typing through three separate drafts.

The book is dedicated to my father, Allan Prentiss, who shared with me his enjoyment of books and politics.

B.H.

Ithaca, N.Y., Fall, 1970

THE

Seniority System

IN

Congress

I

The Seniority System: An Introduction

THE SENIORITY SYSTEM OF CONGRESS has been called by Representative Emanuel Celler "as popular a target as sin itself."[1] The defects of the system have been extensively catalogued for more than two decades with each recurring plea for congressional reform. Yet the seniority system—basically a device for selecting congressional leaders—has not been systematically examined to determine the kinds of leaders it selects, its specific impact on their selection, or the way it functions within the congressional system.[2] Few institutions have been subject to so much attack and so little appraisal.

Its critics contend that the seniority rule, or "senility rule," rewards age and long service and thus builds a generation gap into congressional decision making which gives great power to those least likely to be attuned to contemporary needs.[3] By stipulating long congressional service the seniority system, it is charged, benefits certain one-party areas of the nation at the expense of others, overrepresenting in the committee chairs rural and conservative interests, Democrats from the South and Republicans from the rural Midwest and Northeast.[4] It obstructs party cohesion in Congress by creating independent power centers, a cadre of chairmen not responsible to party leaders since those leaders do not control their selection.[5] And it reinforces this anti-party (and anti-President) tendency by favoring congressmen from safe districts, who are most likely to be out of step with current party programs.[6] In defense of

3

the system it is argued that it avoids the organizational disruption and political in-fighting of other methods of choosing committee heads. In other words, the alternatives would be worse.[7] And yet as recently as 1965 the Joint Committee on the Organization of Congress received *ten* separate major proposals for altering the present system—ranging from the modest proposal of a maximum age limit for chairmen (70 or 72) to selection of chairmen by party leaders or by secret ballot of the majority party committee members at the beginning of each new Congress.[8]

This body of criticism raises important questions concerning the distribution of influence in Senate and House and the functioning of a major congressional institution. Does the seniority system exert a systematic impact on the selection of leaders, overrepresenting some kinds of congressmen and some interests at the expense of others? If so, is length of *congressional* service, stressed by the critics,[9] the principal determinant of leadership? The seniority rule actually refers to length of service on the *committee*, not in Congress; hence original committee assignments, or subsequent changes in committee membership, also affect the selection of leaders. Does the seniority system distribute chairmanships according to pre-existing power alignments, and, if so, what specific alignments? The answers to these questions are not necessarily mutually exclusive. Fundamentally they concern (1) to what extent and in what way the leaders selected are representative of the membership of the congressional party and (2) whether the seniority system per se, and in particular congressional seniority, exerts a systematic selective impact on leadership. The present study will attempt to answer these questions.

Key Characteristics and Historical Development

THE SENIORITY SYSTEM IS A DEVICE FOR SELECTING the leaders of the standing committees. It is a way of ranking members, by party, according to their years of consecutive service on the committee. Parties add or drop members only at the lowest rankings. The seniority system, then, designates the top-ranking member of each party. The senior member whose party gains control of Senate or House becomes the chairman; the senior member from the other party becomes the ranking minority member.

The seniority system is unique to the United States Congress. No other national legislative assemblies, no state legislatures use seniority as the sole criterion for choosing leaders. Representative Udall brought this to the attention of House members:

The answer is none; none except the U.S. Congress. Fifty state legislatures, the British, French, the Swedes, the Australians, no one else uses what we are told is an indispensable system to which we are told there is no alternative.[10]

The "seniority rule" is a custom, not a formal rule of Congress. The rules simply dictate that House or Senate shall determine committee membership and chairmen: "At the commencement of each Congress, the House shall elect as chairman of each standing committee one of the members thereof." Yet despite its lack of formal status, in recent American history exceptions have been made only in extraordinary circumstances. Senators Ladd, Brookhart, Frazier, and La Follette lost their committee seniority in 1925 after bolting the Republican party in the election of 1924.[11] Senator Morse lost his committee seniority (and his committees) in 1953, but Morse had voluntarily left the Republican party and sought committee assignments as an Independent. As the debate on the matter made clear, committee assignments were considered a party's business. In ousting Morse from his old positions, the Republicans could argue that they were simply following the seniority rule for their party members.[12] The deposition of Adam Clayton Powell, a Democrat, from the chairmanship of the House Education Committee came only after Powell had not only supported a Republican presidential candidate but also, in many observers' eyes, violated a number of other congressional standards. During the past forty years, many others—Progressive Republicans and Southern Democrats particularly—have bolted the party during presidential elections, thus violating the minimum criterion of party loyalty. But few of them have lost committee seniority in subsequent Congresses.[13] Even against such strains in party loyalty as these, the seniority rule has held firm.

The rule is strongly reinforced by the tradition of respect for seniority in Congress. It is part of the "seniority-protégé-apprentice system," to use Richard Fenno's phrase, for minimizing conflict over who shall exercise influence and who shall not.[14] This affects all congressmen, not merely those in line for chairmanships. Respect for seniority affects the choice of committee assignments, assignment of office space, recognition on the floor and in committee hearings, as well as committee chairmanships.

The historical development of the seniority system in House and Senate throws further light on the present situation. To summarize only the highlights, in the nineteenth century seniority was only one of a number of criteria governing the selection of chairmen. The seniority rule grew stronger as legislation became more complex, leading to pressures for specialization and "professionalization"; at the same time House and Senate careers were growing longer.[15] One can find a firm seniority principle at work in the Senate between 1885 and 1895, although it had become a generally accepted rule even before the Civil War.[16] Despite a slower growth in the junior chamber, there was an erratic but continuing increase in the number of times seniority was followed in the selection of House chairmen from 1881 through 1910. The seniority principle gained strength as the Speaker's control over appointments was undermined with the Republicans in 1910 and with the Democrats in 1919,[17] and after the House's unsuccessful experimentation with more centralized leadership seniority emerged as the single automatic criterion for selecting chairmen. The slower growth of seniority in the House may have been due more in part to that chamber's need for more centralized leadership concentrated in the Speaker, because of its larger size and diversity. A second reason for the slower growth of seniority in the House may have been that age and expertise were less venerated than in the Senate. ("Senate" and "seniority" have the same Latin base, *senex,* meaning "old.") The nineteenth-century House elected young Speakers, the most notable being Henry Clay, elected Speaker on his first day as a member. Further, membership turnover in the House in the nineteenth century was extremely rapid. Many districts deliberately rotated their Representatives, agreeing with Andrew Jackson that democracy required a constant change of leaders to avoid the dangers of oligarchy, and believing also that a House seat was "a good thing which should be passed around."[18] From his vantage point at the turn of the century, Woodrow Wilson contrasts the routes to leadership in the two houses:

Leaders of the Senate . . . are generally men of long training in public affairs who have been under inspection by their fellow members for many sessions together. The Senate is inclined to follow its veterans . . . who by long service have gained a full experience. . . . The leaders of the House win their places . . . in a restless and changeful assembly few of whose members remain in the public service long enough to know any men's qualities intimately.[19]

One need only apply Wilson's characterization of the "restless and changeful assembly" to the contemporary House of Representatives to see the dramatic change since Wilson's day. As House membership grew more stable through the end of the nineteenth and beginning of the twentieth century,[20] support for the seniority principle grew stronger.

This gradual change in the character of House and Senate helps to explain the historical development of the seniority system. If this is true, then the contemporary composition of the two houses may help to explain the contemporary working of the system as well. For despite all the criticism from within

Congress and from outside, the system continues to be used. Something must be supporting it.

The Products of the System—The Chairmen

WHAT KINDS OF MEN BECOME CHAIRMEN UNDER the seniority system? A brief sketch of some of them may be useful. To gain some sense of the range and variety among chairmen, two Congresses—one Republican and one Democratic—can be used for illustration. These two Congresses, the 83rd and the 87th, both found a new President and new party in the White House. Who were some of the chairmen?

Among Senate Republicans heading committees as the GOP gained control of the first Eisenhower (83rd) Congress were such northeastern liberal Republicans as Leverett Saltonstall, 61, of Massachusetts (Armed Services) and George Aiken, 61, of Vermont (Agriculture). Both chaired important and prestigious committees. However, other committees were headed by such staunch Taft supporters as Millikin of Colorado, 62 (Finance), and Bridges of New Hampshire, 55 (Appropriations). Two of Eisenhower's biggest headaches originated with chairmen. Bricker of Ohio chaired the Commerce Committee and sponsored the proposed Bricker Amendment. And chairman of the Government Operations Committee was 45-year-old Joe McCarthy of Wisconsin. Altogether, of the fifteen Senate chairmen, ten were from the Midwest, four from the East, and one from the West. Ages ranged from 45 to 75.

Among the House Democratic chairmen in the 87th (Kennedy) Congress, the Rules Committee was chaired by 78-year-old "Judge" Howard Smith of Virginia, noted for his conservatism, legislative ability, and "iron control" of his committee. Clarence Cannon of Missouri, 82, parliamentarian and "crusty loner" according to Representative Bolling,[21] headed the powerful Appropriations Committee, as he had done except for brief Republican interludes since 1941. The third of the most powerful House committees—Ways and Means—was chaired by 52-year-old Wilbur Mills. Mills was born in Arkansas, educated at Harvard Law School, and admired for his lucid explanations of complicated bills on the House floor.

Another extremely influential House chairman was Carl Vinson, 78, of Georgia, Chairman of the Armed Services Committee. Vinson was noted for his control in committee, for his ability to get unanimous committee votes on controversial legislation, and for his influence throughout the House and in the Department of Defense. The story is told that when the new Department of Defense was created in the Truman Administration it was suggested that Vinson would make a good Secretary of Defense. According to the story, Vinson returned, "Shucks, I'd rather run the Pentagon from up here." Recognized as a key man on votes where Southerners might not follow party lines, Vinson was to play a major role in helping pass controversial legislation. According to Bolling, Vinson was on the Kennedy team. "My God," someone remarked after the 87th Congress was well under way, "Vinson even made a New Frontier speech down home in Georgia."[22]

A key House committee in the Kennedy Congress, where civil rights legislation would be shaped, was Judiciary, chaired by Emanuel Celler, 73, of New York. New York had the largest contingent of chairmen—three. The two other chairmen from New York were Adam Clayton Powell, 53, of Education and Labor; and Charles Buckley, 71, of Public Works. The Democratic chairmen included two Negroes—Powell and William Dawson of Government Operations, a machine politician from the south side of Chicago. The Southern predominence was apparent not only in the three most prestigious House committees. The Veterans Committee was headed by Teague of Texas; Merchant Marine, by Bonner of North Carolina; House Un-American Activities Committee by Walter of Pennsylvania; and House Administration by Burleson of Texas. Eleven of the twenty chairmen were Southerners. Ages ranged from 51 to 87.

Even this brief sketch should give some sense of the variety of men who become chairmen. And yet one can certainly appreciate the critics' point of the "perversity" of the seniority system. Dwight Eisenhower came to the White House with sufficiently strong electoral support to allow the Republicans to gain control of Congress, on a platform of "Modern Republicanism." To most observers, this suggested something quite different from the "Old Guard" Republicanism and its opposition to the New Deal, now almost twenty years old. The Old Guard Republicans, moreover, with Senator Robert Taft as their spokesman, had just lost the Republican presidential nomination. But as the "Modern Republican" Administration looked across to Capitol Hill, there were Senators Joe McCarthy, William Knowland, Eugene Millikin, and others managing the committee business. To take another example, John F. Kennedy came to the presidency calling for the energy of a New Frontier to be created by men "born in this century." But as the young liberal Administration looked to Congress, they found 78-year-old Smith of Virginia, 82-year-old Cannon, and 78-year-old Vinson in the committee chairs.

But what was the rest of the Congress like? And what other kinds of leadership were available? The Majority Leader in the Senate in the first Eisenhower Administration was Taft, accepted leader of the Old Guard. On Taft's death, William Knowland became Majority Leader, although he admittedly found the job of presidential spokesman in the Senate in serious conflict with certain deeply held conservative principles. And the New Frontier had as presidential spokesman in the House Speaker Sam Rayburn of Texas, the most senior man in the House.

Dramatic contrasts between Presidents and chairmen do not explain the more fundamental contrast between the presidency and Congress. To put the seniority system in its proper setting, we must examine not only the committee chairmen but Congress as a whole.

Influences on the Selection of Chairmen

A NUMBER OF FACTORS, INCLUDING SENIORITY, MAY
determine the selection of committee chairmen. First, the
distribution of members in a congressional party may set
important limits. If 50 per cent of the Senate Democrats
are Southerners, then Democratic committee leaders might
well include 50 per cent Southerners, even if the choice
were by lot. Second, as much of the commentary suggests,
long service in Congress—*congressional seniority,* as required by the seniority rule—might well influence the selection of chairmen. Third, *committee assignments,* both
initial appointments and subsequent transfers to more
desirable committees, can affect committee seniority. Finally,
what Joseph Clark calls the *"luck of the seniority draw"*[23]
may exert a major impact. If several senior members of
a committee die, resign, or shift assignments, a relatively
junior man may gain rank quickly. Similarly, a fairly senior man
may have the misfortune to be ranked below one or two ex-
ceptionally hardy men with even greater seniority. Such factors
as the size of the committee or the tenacity of other committee
members can operate quite independently of congressional
seniority. Consider the case of John Sparkman in the 88th Congress, sixteen years in the Senate, sixteen years on the Banking
and Currency Committee. He outranked many chairmen on
these two seniority counts, but was nevertheless only second
on the committee, ranked behind an even more senior Democrat—A. Willis Robertson of Virginia. (He was second also on
Foreign Relations, again outranked by a more senior Southerner—J. W. Fulbright.)

Conventional criticism of the subject usually concentrates on
one factor only—the influence of congressional seniority. The
seniority system, it is said, by rewarding long congressional
service, effectively denies chairmanships to those states and
districts that do not regularly return incumbents to office. One

can see the result in the safe-seat, Southern Democratic over-representation in the committee chairs. This formulation is a plausible one, and well worth investigation.

Another interpretation is possible, however, and it is explored in this study. It may be that the seniority requirement exerts only a marginal impact on the choice of congressional leaders, given the stability over time of American voters' party loyalties, the resulting stability of congressional membership, and the variety of congressional career patterns. This suggests that (1) committee leaders may reflect in a general way the distribution of the members of their congressional party and that (2) where "misrepresentation" does occur, it may be attributable as much to patterns of committee assignment and committee changes as to congressional seniority. Therefore, the kind of chairmen selected may be the result of many causes, with the seniority rule only one of a number of influences, and in the traditional criticism its impact may have been considerably overstated.

The conventional emphasis on congressional seniority echoes the older notion of a truly competitive party system, where strong and persistent competition between parties at the state and district levels and frequent turnover of candidates is the normal situation, and one-party constituencies are abnormal. By this older notion, the seniority system rewards the abnormal minority at the expense of the majority and poses a serious conflict between the turnover encouraged by the party system and the continuity encouraged by the seniority system. But the majority of states and districts are *not* subject to frequent election overturns. American voters show marked stability in party loyalties—tending to vote for the same party for different offices over a number of elections.[24] Moreover, in elections for both the House and Senate incumbents have a decided advantage over their challengers. Senate and House incumbents of both parties over the past decade have averaged 85 per cent victories in their fights for reelection.[25] Both effects combine to

12

produce an extremely stable congressional membership. Once in office a congressman tends to stay.

In a legislative body where long service is not the exception but the rule, a stipulation for long service is not especially restrictive. It screens out only that small fraction of states and districts which, unlike the majority, are marked by frequent turnover in party control.

Second, when shifts in party fortunes at congressional elections do occur—in both presidential-year and midterm elections—they tend to occur in the same general direction in line with national trends. They may be results of a strong presidential vote in presidential-year elections, or of a derivative countertendency* at midterm elections, or of changes in party loyalties spread over an extensive regional, interest, or ideological base. In any case, they produce a clear swing for or against a party's congressional candidates rather than merely an aggregate result of many idiosyncratic contests.[26] Such large and clear trends are reflected in the membership of the congressional party—producing for example a relative increase in midwestern Democrats vis-à-vis Southern Democrats—and, over time, affect the chairmanships. This effect is attributable not to congressional seniority but to the fact that there are relatively more congressmen of one kind than of other kinds within a congressional party. The key to understanding how committee leaders are selected may, then, be the composition of the party's membership in Congress. The larger the number of Southern Senate Democrats in relation to Senate Democrats from other regions, the larger the relative number of committee posts they may be expected to receive.

A third point which casts doubt on the overriding importance of congressional seniority is the variety exhibited by congres-

---

* The automatic loss of the seats won by the help of the presidential vote two years before. See Barbara Hinckley in *American Political Science Review,* September 1967.

sional career patterns. Many different goals can be pursued by the ambitious congressman, only one of which is a committee chairmanship. Others include a place in the party leadership, a firm interest base from which to deal with one's constituency politics, or a base allowing one to pursue the role of maverick critic of government policies.[27] It follows that rank on a specific committee would be valued differently depending on the individual's personal goal and strategy. It may suit some congressmen to stay on one committee to gain the chairmanship. Others may prefer to change committee assignments in pursuit of their individual goals or at the suggestion of the party leadership. These variations will have no necessary relationship to congressional seniority.

All this indicates that the selection of committee leaders is a much more complicated process than the usual arguments would suggest. If so, investigation should reveal (1) evidence of a variety of representational patterns for House and Senate, Democrats and Republicans, varying with differences in membership and patterns of factional strength; and (2) in cases where over- or underrepresentation is observable, evidence that it is not solely due to congressional seniority.

Scope and Limits of the Study

THIS STUDY, THEN, ATTEMPTS A SYSTEMATIC ANALYsis of the seniority system with particular attention to its capacity to select leaders who are representative of their congressional party. It attempts to extricate the effects of the system, particularly the requirement of long congressional service, from other influences affecting the kind of chairmen selected. The strategy for analysis is as follows. First, the four congressional parties are examined to see what kind of action may be expected at a given time in a given congressional party, not simply what may be expected from the Southern Democrats who happened to hold chairmanships in the past two decades. Second, within each party, committee leaders are compared with the full congressional party membership, the "senior" membership, and the "committee seniors," in an attempt to isolate points of influence on the final selection of chairmen.

The main focus of attention is on the chairmen and ranking minority members (the "shadow chairmen")—altogether the 40 Senate Democrats, 51 House Democrats, 46 Senate Republicans, and 71 House Republicans who headed the standing committees of Congress during the twenty-year span from 1947 through 1966. Ranking minority members are sufficiently secure electorally speaking to allow them a place in the comparison. A "senior" will be defined by length of consecutive congressional service, the definition varying with the congressional party. No one definition of seniority can meaningfully be applied across the four congressional parties. A "committee senior" will be defined as a congressional senior who either stayed on at least one committee of initial appointment or, if elected before 1946, stayed on at least one committee he was appointed to following the 1946 Legislative Reorganization Act's revision of the committee structure.[28] A later chapter will compare committee chairmen and party leaders.

These data provide a reliable description of various patterns of representation in Congress. Members of Congress are classified by their age and congressional seniority; by the electoral "safeness" and regional and demographic characteristics of their constituencies; by their support for party and presidential programs; and by the "liberalism" or "conservatism" of their voting records. These diverse classifications permit considerable flexibility in comparing the four congressional parties and in pinpointing possible different kinds of influence in the selection of chairmen.

The period chosen, 1947–1966, covers almost the full span of the modern committee structure set by the 1946 Reorganization Act. One major part of the investigation is based on patterns formed over the full time span, since we are dealing with a process that occurs over time, and since a shorter time span would rule out analysis of the Senate, whose full membership is subject to change only once in six years. Separate investigations for single Congresses are included where relevant. Brief accounts of patterns existing before 1946 are included for comparative purposes.

Some limits of the study should be made clear at the outset. The concept of "representativeness" raises a host of problems of definition, of evidence, and of interpretation. "Representativeness" is here defined simply as *proportionality*, a correspondence in distribution between two or more groups.[29] The ideal is assumed to be an exact correspondence between the thing represented and the representative, as in the "one-man-one-vote" standard for apportionment. Although the group to be represented by the chairmen is not made explicit in the commentaries, it is taken in this study to refer to the members of the congressional party. The assumption is that all that can be expected of an ideally representative group of chairmen is that they reflect the proportions of their congressional party membership in certain important respects. If the Republicans can elect no Southerners to the Senate, Republican Senate chairmen cannot be expected to "represent" the South.

While the salient characteristics selected as a necessary first step in this investigation—such as age, safeness of the seat, region, support of the President, and liberal or conservative voting—may not tell the whole story of a chairman's "representativeness," they are stressed in the traditional criticism and are perceived by congressmen themselves to be important. Note criticisms of the "Southern-biased" seniority system or attempts to "liberalize" the Democratic Steering Committee or Rules Committee.

Neither measurement nor interpretation is easy, however. How much deviation from a one-to-one correspondence can be

16

permitted? How much is "unrepresentative"? The point is important, for no one measure can be exclusively relied on without creating rigid categories which would distort the results. Further, some of the strongest evidence may come from the kind of situation that is not susceptible to precise measurement at all. Accordingly a wide range of quantitative and nonquantitative evidence will be presented. Essentially, the interpretation rests on some thirty tables showing profiles of representativeness as defined by a number of criteria, and nonquantitative evidence of similarities and differences among congressmen and patterns of interaction and support. While the author cannot shrug off the task of interpretation, the reader is invited to make interpretations of his own.

The difficulties of interpretation, of course, arise from the political nature of the subject matter. The seniority system has been defined, or "dramatized" may be the better word, by its critics, who have also been critics of Congress's legislative record over the past twenty years and critics of a system of separated powers which moves often too slowly and sometimes does not move at all. Thus it may seem an easy step from dissatisfaction with the outcome of Kennedy's tax reform proposal to dissatisfaction with Wilbur Mills, and from there to criticism of the system that made him chairman of Ways and Means. Such reasoning omits the key factor of what the House Democrats as a whole thought about tax reform. Presumably the same system might work the other way. If, in the future, Northern liberal Democrats begin to climb their committee ladders more quickly, as some of the data suggest may be the case, the oldtime liberal critics may rally to the seniority system's defense. The subject has been used as a talking point for launching attempts at congressional reform or for expressing dissatisfaction with particular legislative results. From the day the first Senator rose on the floor of the Senate in 1859 to denounce the system of seniority that was giving chairmanships to all the slave-holding states[30] to the time at the end of the nine-

17

teenth century when its Northern-state bias was blamed on "Yankee tenacity and longevity,"[31] and down to the present, the seniority system has been denounced from various standpoints. But it has not been studied for itself and for what it shows about how leaders are selected in Congress.

This is the concern of the present study.

II

The Concept of "Seniority"

$\mathbf{M}$UCH OF THE CONFUSION surrounding the subject may stem from the vagueness of the concept of "seniority." It suggests time spent, tenure; in this context, some number of years consecutive service in Congress or on a committee. But how many years are necessary to be considered "senior"? And how much does seniority vary from one congressional party to another depending on the turnover of members? In a young party one might become a senior in six years, whereas in an old one even a ten-year man may attract little veneration. How closely related are congressional and committee seniority? A number of assumptions about the seniority system depend for their validity on answers to such simple questions. Consider the stereotype of "the little group of committee chairmen who were first elected to Congress a generation ago on issues now settled and forgotten," making decisions on legislation they can no longer understand.[1] Or consider the assertion that the system screens out a majority of states and districts from the chance at a chairmanship, which requires comparison of the average congressional service of chairmen before attaining leadership with the average length of service of all members of Congress.

This chapter supplies some substantive meaning to the word "seniority" by defining it in terms of (1) the age, tenure, and congressional careers of committee leaders (chairmen and ranking minority members); (2) the congressional seniority possessed by these leaders compared with the full membership; and (3) the relationship between congressional and committee seniority.

Age and Length of Service

TO BEGIN WITH A FACT THAT WILL SURPRISE NO ONE, committee leaders are indeed "senior" in age. The median age for committee chairmen and ranking minority members for the years 1947–66 comes close to what is considered the standard retirement age in this society. The median age for Senate Democratic committee leaders is 66; for House Democrats, 65.5; for Senate Republicans, 63.5; and for House Republicans, 62.3.[2] This age level is slightly higher than the median age of all Senate and House members. The median age for Senators ranges between 55 and 60; for Representatives between 50 and 55.[3] It is interesting to note that if Congress had followed the recurring suggestion of a maximum age limit such as 70 for chairmen, a large number of committee leaders would have been disqualified. Seventeen Democratic Senators, 19 Democratic Representatives, 11 Republican Senators, and 20 Republican Representatives would have been automatically retired from their posts.

A second part of this temporal definition, however, may be much more surprising. The conventional view suggests that a chairmanship is a prize which only the hardiest—physically and electorally—can aspire to. But the number of years it takes a congressman to gain top committee rank from his first entry into the House or Senate varies considerably from one party and chamber to the other. The median years required to gain top rank for the chairmen and ranking minority members of 1947 through 1966 are as follows:[4]

Senate Democrats 10
House Democrats 16
Senate Republicans 7
House Republicans 12

Approximately this number of years is sufficient to gain top rank on the majority of committees. Committees requiring more than the median number of years include not only the more prestigious, such as Appropriations, Ways and Means, Foreign Relations, and Armed Services, but some low-ranking committees also, such as Post Office, Labor, Government Operations, and House Un-American Activities Committees.[5] According to the Miller-Stokes six-level ranking of House committees by prestige, only Democratic chairmen of committees in the top level of prestige and those in the lowest level show any clear difference in years of previous congressional service. No clear difference is apparent for House Republican leaders.[6]

If one translates these findings into the number of elections that must be won along the way, House Democrats on the average must win nine elections and House Republicans seven to qualify for a post, whereas in the Senate, both Democrats and Republicans need win only two.

These facts suggest that the usual jump in the literature from seniority to electoral safeness may be much too hastily made. In the Senate, by this criterion of number of elections won, forty-eight states could have had at least one chairman or ranking minority member in 1947–1966. (Alaska and Hawaii would not qualify.) And in the House, although the requirement of seven to nine elections seems more severe, the number of congressional districts which could meet this requirement is rather large. In the twenty-year span, 198 Democratic congressional districts and 139 Republican districts fulfilled the minimum requirement of remaining under the same party banner for at least the nine and seven consecutive elections of the average requirement. So of the 435 present districts, only 22 per cent would be automatically excluded. As operationally defined by the experience of these twenty years, the time required to gain seniority excludes only the two states new to statehood and only 22 per cent of the congressional districts from Senate and House committee leadership.

A third finding may also be surprising. The number of years

a chairman or ranking minority member stays in his top committee position may be shorter than is commonly thought. The median number of years for Senate Democrats is 8; for House Democrats, 6; for Senate Republicans, 4; and for House Republicans, 6. Thus committee leadership, according to Joseph Schlesinger's classification, would be called an "intermediate" office—too short to qualify as a "career" office and too long to be called a "transitory" office.[7] Any view of the venerable chairman, outlasting President after President, is not supported by these facts. Presidents, it would seem, do just as well or better than the average committee chairman or ranking minority member. A few committee chairmen, of course, correspond to the conventional image—for example, Senate Democrat George (21 years), House Republicans Taber (30 years) and Hope (24 years). The record-holder is House Democrat Carl Vinson, Committee Chairman or ranking minority member of Naval Affairs or Armed Services for 42 years. The number of years congressmen occupy top committee posts is given in Table 1. The

TABLE 1.   NUMBER OF YEARS CONGRESSMEN SERVED AS COMMITTEE CHAIRMEN OR RANKING MINORITY MEMBERS, 1947–66[a]

	NUMBER OF CONGRESSMEN			
NO. OF YEARS AS CC OR RMM	SENATE *Dem.*	HOUSE *Dem.*	SENATE *Rep.*	HOUSE *Rep.*
More than 20	1	4	0	3
13—20	5	6	2	7
5—12	10	11	12	20
4 or less	9	11	17	25
Total no. of congressmen	**25**	**32**	**31**	**55**

a. Only those congressmen whose terms were completed by 1965-66 are included.

figures show that, although a few members serve lengthy terms —and those are the giants who come to mind—all the rest remain in office much more briefly.

To give some substance to the notion of the "time lag" built into committee leadership, one can specify the rate of turnover in committee posts per decade; i.e., what proportion of chairmen and ranking minority members who held rank at the beginning of a decade had left by the end of it. The results given in Table 2 cover the past four decades.[8]

TABLE 2.   RATE OF TURNOVER OF COMMITTEE LEADERS BY DECADE, 1921–60

	COMMITTEE LEADERS WHO LEFT OFFICE DURING THE DECADE (PER CENT)			
	SENATE *Dem.*	HOUSE *Dem.*	SENATE *Rep.*	HOUSE *Rep.*
1921–30	33	39	52	52
1931–40	39	56	47	67
1941–50	53	39	50	42
1951–60	44	42	50	58

Roughly, more than 40 per cent of the committee leaders on the average change within one decade, with the most recent ten years registering a mean turnover rate of all congressional parties of close to 50 per cent. But the *variety* in the turnover rate among the four congressional parties for any one decade, and especially the variety between House and Senate leaders of the same party, should be noticed. Compare the 47 and 67 per cent rates for the Republicans in the 1930's and the 39 and 56 per cent rates for the Democrats in the 1930's. In view of this variety, no one average figure for time lag should be used without considerable caution. Perhaps all one can say is that it has taken about a decade or slightly more to change a majority of the committee leaders.

Such intraparty differences in the same decade suggest that a party's electoral popularity does not significantly affect the rate of turnover. During the "Republican" 1920's, Republican chairmen in both House and Senate changed more frequently than the Democrats. In the "Democratic" 1940's, Senate Democratic chairmen changed more frequently than Senate Republicans. And the highest rate of turnover of House Democrats also came in the 1940's. In only one case did electoral defeat seem substantially to influence the rate of turnover. Seventeen

Republican ranking minority members were defeated in the decade of the 1930's, producing the highest rate of turnover registered for any of the congressional parties in the four decades.

Even though Republicans have suffered more electoral defeats than Democrats, the total number of committee leaders of each party leaving involuntarily—that is, through death or defeat in a primary or general election, as opposed to through retirement—is almost the same, as Table 3 makes clear.

TABLE 3.   INTERPARTY SIMILARITY IN INVOLUNTARY RETIREMENT, 1947–66[a]

COMMITTEE LEADERS	No.	No. Who Left by Election Defeat	No. Who Left by Primary Defeat	No. Who Left by Election or Primary Defeat or Death
Senate Democrats	40	1	2	10
Senate Republicans	46	7	0	9
House Democrats	51	1	3	15
House Republicans	71	6	1	15

a. The higher incidence of primary defeat among Democrats helps to even the numbers of congressmen leaving through "involuntary retirement," but does not fully explain the similarity between parties of the numbers in the right-hand column. The similarity seems to be produced by the action of a nonpolitical variable. In this case, as the saying goes, death appears to be the "great leveler." Democrats, with lower incidence of defeat, had a higher incidence of death in the committee chairs.

It is possible that some proportion of those who retired *voluntarily* did so because they read the writing on the wall—an electoral situation which spelled defeat in the primary or election. The analysis here cannot probe this possibility. If such is the case, the higher incidence of voluntary retirement among Republicans might indicate some additional electoral vulnerability. (Those who left top committee posts by voluntary retirement are as follows: Senate Democrats, 14; Senate Republicans, 21; House Democrats, 16; and House Republicans, 36.)

Congressional Seniority

THE IMPACT OF THE SENIORITY SYSTEM MAY WELL hinge on the restrictiveness of the congressional tenure requirement—that is, on what proportion of congressmen it disqualifies from the selection process. If the requirement can be defined as the average number of consecutive elections which must be won before receiving a top committee post, the preceding section supplies data with which to investigate this alleged restrictiveness.

The range of the tenure requirement across the four congressional parties—from two consecutive elections for Senators to nine for House Democrats—obviously prohibits the use of any one measure as a definition of what constitutes a congressional "senior." But it seems suitable to take as an operational definition for each congressional party how many consecutive elections had to be won to gain a ranking position on a committee in more than half of the cases in the past two decades: two consecutive elections for Senate Democrats and Republicans; seven for House Republicans; and nine for House Democrats. (Since the Senate Democrats took an average of ten years, a full Congress more than the minimum seven years, to have won two consecutive elections, it seems necessary to add the requirement for Senate Democrats, unnecessary in the other three cases, that they have not only won two consecutive elections but also served at least ten years.) For an alternate, stricter definition, to be used as a check in subsequent inquiries, one can take the number of consecutive elections won in three-fourths to all of the cases: three consecutive elections for Senate Democrats and Republicans; nine for House Republicans; and eleven for House Democrats. These definitions form the basis for identification of congressional "seniors" and "advanced seniors" as used throughout the study.

This congressional seniority requirement, thus defined, should be viewed within the general context of congressional electoral patterns. As suggested earlier, the overall stability in the electorate's party attachments can be expected to produce an overall stability in congressional membership, and thus for the average congressman an expectation of considerable tenure. The normal situation, especially in House districts, is not a competitive one, as a number of writers have pointed out.[9] Incumbent candidates for both Senate and House—exhibiting an average 85 per cent success rate—have a decided advantage over nonincumbents.

The Senate requirement of two consecutive victories and even the House requirement of seven to nine consecutive victories may not, therefore, be a very stiff hurdle. Of the forty-eight states examined during the twenty-year span, only four did not have a least two "senior" Senators, using the preceding definitions of a "senior" for each party. Oregon, Wyoming, and Kentucky had one senior each, and Connecticut had none. (Senator Dodd of Connecticut had won two consecutive elections, but by 1966 had not yet served ten years.) Six states had three seniors. All the remaining thirty-eight had more than three. In contradiction to the claim that the seniority system penalizes competitive states, these data suggest that at the senatorial level few states are very competitive. Parties may divide the two Senate seats, but the two seats themselves are "safe" for the incumbents.[10] In the House, despite the apparent stiffness of the requirement of seven to nine consecutive elections won, from 1947 to 1966 fifty-one separate House Democrats attained the position of committee chairman or ranking minority member, while more than twice that number (139) "qualified" by winning nine consecutive elections.[11] The seniority rule, in other words, stipulates long service from a membership where long service is not the exception but the rule.

It is, of course, true that the more congressional seniority a congressman possesses the better his chances are for receiving a top committee post. Yet some interesting discontinuities are evident. If committee leadership were strictly determined by congressional seniority, one would expect that all chairmanships would be held by the members with the longest service and, conversely, that no members would hold chairmanships while some outranking them in congressional tenure did not. Analysis of the membership of two Congresses, the 85th(1957–58) and the 88th (1963–64), illustrates the discontinuities found to exist throughout the twenty-year span. The results for the Senate are given in Table 4 and for the House in Table 5.

The tables show in varying degrees some relationship be-

TABLE 4. RELATIONSHIP BETWEEN CONGRESSIONAL SENIORITY
AND COMMITTEE LEADERSHIP: SENATE, 1957–58, 1963–64[a]

CONGRESSIONAL SENIORITY: No. Years Continuous Service	DEMOCRATS			REPUBLICANS		
	SENS. No.	CC'S No.	CC'S %	SENS. No.	RMM'S No.	RMM'S %
			1957–58			
20 or more	7	7	100	1	1	100
15—19	1	1	100	3	2	67
10—14	10	5	50	16	6	38
5—9	14	2	14	9	2	22
0—4	17	0	0	19	2	11
Total	49	15		48	13	
			1963–64			
20 or more	7	7	100	1	1	100
15—19	9	4	45	5	4	80
10—14	11	2	18	7	7	100
5—9	10	2	20	8	3	38
0—4	31	1	3	11	0	0
Total	68	16		32	15	

a. Number of years of continuous service measures the seniority accumulated as of the beginning of the term in 1957 and 1963. For both Congresses, the number of Republican ranking minority members is lower than the number of Democratic chairmen because some Republicans serve as ranking minority members on more than one committee.

tween the two "hierarchies," but the relationship is by no means a strict one. Considerable discontinuities are evident. To turn to the Senate first, one finds the strongest correspondence among the 1957–58 Democrats. All of the Senators who had served fifteen years or more had chairmanships. Five of the ten Senators serving ten to fifteen years had chairmanships. And only two Senators (in the five-to-nine-year category) held chairs which, if congressional seniority were strictly followed, would have gone to men in the ten-to-fourteen-year category who were not chairmen. For the Democrats in 1963–64 and the Republicans in both Congresses, the correspondence is less strong. It is true that the most senior Senators (those serving twenty years or more) all had chairmanships, but below that top category considerable discontinuity is evident, as can be seen by reading down the columns and noting the number of Senators who received top committee positions in each category while members outranking them in congressional seniority did not.

An interesting subsidiary question can be raised: who are the Senators thus bypassed for top-ranking committee positions? The usual argument that the seniority system has a "regional bias," particularly in the Democatic party a Southern bias," might suggest that it would be the non-Southern Democrats who were bypassed for committee posts. But if anything, the opposite is the case. In 1957–58 five Democrats serving ten to fourteen years were not chairmen, while two of shorter service were. Excluding Wayne Morse of Oregon, who lost his seniority by switching parties, the four "bypassed" Senators were all from Southern states: Holland of Florida, Robertson of Virginia, Sparkman of Alabama, and Long of Louisiana. The two Senate chairmen who were more junior in congressional tenure were both from border states: Neely of West Virginia and Hennings of Missouri. In 1963–64 five Senators serving fifteen to nineteen years were not chairmen. Excepting Wayne Morse, they were all Southerners: again, Sparkman, Holland, and Long, and also Stennis of Mississippi. Of the five chairmen below them in congressional seniority who were benefited, only two were from the South.

The results for the House are similar to those in the Senate. Some relationship is evident between the two hierarchies, but not a particularly strong one. The House, of course, is a considerably larger body and has more members who have served more than twenty years. A category was added to the table for the House to distinguish members who had served twenty to twenty-four years from those who had served more than twenty-four. With only nineteen or twenty committee chairs available, there were not enough chairmanships to distribute among all the veteran members. Even so, the allocation by no means closely followed congressional seniority. Some of the most senior members in the House were bypassed for the top committee posts among both Democrats and Republicans in both Congresses. Reading down the columns in Table 5 in decreasing order of congressional seniority, one finds in both parties and in both Congresses a considerable number of Representatives without top committee posts while more junior congressmen received them.

TABLE 5. RELATIONSHIP BETWEEN CONGRESSIONAL SENIORITY AND COMMITTEE LEADERSHIP: HOUSE OF REPRESENTATIVES, 1957–58, 1963–64

CONGRESSIONAL SENIORITY: No. Years Continuous Service	DEMOCRATS			REPUBLICANS		
	REPS. No.	CC'S No.	CC'S %	REPS. No.	RMM'S No.	RMM'S %
1957–58						
More than 24	9[a]	5	56	7	4	57
20—24	17	4	24	8	4	50
15—19	17	4	24	19	5	26
10—14	42	6	14	41	6	15
5—9	42	0	0	42	0	0
0—4	80	0	0	68	0	0
Total	207	19		185	19	
1963–64						
More than 24	17[b]	7	41	3	2	67
20—24	24	6	25	9	6	67
15—19	24	5	21	8	4	50
10—14	48	2	4	43	5	12
5—9	36	0	0	22	1	5
0—4	91	0	0	84	0	0
Total	240	20		169	18	

a. Two of the four representatives who were not chairmen were Speaker Rayburn and Majority Leader McCormack.

b. One of the ten representatives who were not chairmen was Speaker McCormack.

For the House as for the Senate, the pattern of selection through which committee leadership deviates from congressional seniority does not benefit Southern Democrats. In 1957–58 the two Representatives serving more than twenty-four years who did not have chairmanships (excluding Speaker Rayburn and Majority Leader McCormack) were both from the South: Cooper of Tennessee and Patman of Texas. Of the thirteen next in rank in congressional seniority who did not have chairmanships, seven were from the South. Of that nine in 1963–64 who had served more than twenty-four years and who were thus far bypass~d for chairmen (excluding McCormack), five were from the South.

Committee Seniority

CAN VARIATIONS IN COMMITTEE SENIORITY HELP TO explain these discrepancies? In other words, does the committee seniority requirement exert an independent influence? The seniority system ranks congressmen by consecutive service on the committees. Thus a change of committee reduces a congressman to the bottom rung on the committee ladder. Perhaps some considerable number of congressmen of advanced service in Congress are disqualified for a chairmanship by such a committee change. In all subsequent discussion, a "committee senior" is a "senior" congressman who has stayed on at least one committee of initial assignment or, if elected before 1946, has stayed on the committee assigned following the Legislative Reorganization Act.

The results varied by congressional party so much that no single answer is possible. But some clarification can be offered.

First of all, changing committees is a sufficiently frequent occurrence to merit attention as a possible major influence on results. This statement holds for three of the four congressional parties—the House Democrats and Republicans, and the Senate Republicans—not for the Senate Democrats. Taking all congressmen who began service in or after 1947 and who stayed long enough to be considered "senior" in their congressional party, the percentage of congressmen who changed committees during that time—i.e., did not stay on at least one committee of initial appointment—is as follows:

	% Changing Committees
SD (N=34)	15
HD (N=35)	54
SR (N=25)	40
HR (N=59)	41

Only among the Senate Democrats, where only 15 per cent changed committees, does it seem that "committee hopping" is an infrequent occurrence.

Second, most chairmen and ranking minority members have not changed committees; they have stayed with at least one committee of initial assignment. This may suggest that a committee change seriously hurts one's chances for a top committee post. Again, this is clearly true for three of the congressional parties, somewhat less clearly for the fourth. Investigation of the chairmen and ranking minority members from 1957 on who were "committee seniors" as previously defined—those who did not change committees—showed the following results:

CC's/RMM's	*% Who Stayed with Committee of First Assignment*
SD (N=23)	91
HD (N=27)	93
SR (N=27)	70
HR (N=50)	86

Democratic committee leaders in both Senate and House have stayed with their initial assignment almost without exception. In fact, the two House Democrats who switched and still became chairmen chaired only the House Un-American Activities Committee—a committee marked by frequent turnover and low congressional seniority in its chairmen. House Republicans show a similarly high proportion. Of the seven who switched and still gained a top committee post, three headed the Un-American Activities Committee. Only for the Senate Republicans is the case not so clear, although a still substantial proportion—70 per cent—were committee seniors. This congressional party, of course, suffered the most rapid electoral turnover in the predominantly Democratic years under review and showed the shortest length of congressional service necessary to gain top rank. It thus seems likely that, given the smaller membership and more frequent turnover, a Republican Senator could more easily change committee and still qualify after a short time for committee leadership.

The committee seniority requirement can, then, exert an influence of its own—most clearly for House Democrats and Republicans and, wherever the infrequent committee hopping occurred, for the Senate Democrats also. The extent of this influence will be explored more fully in later chapters. But if, as with congressional seniority, there are *still* more congressmen of advanced congressional service *and* committee seniority than there are committee leadership posts, then one must look outside the seniority system—to the discretion or luck involved in the original committee assignment.

Indications of both influences can be seen in the case of those bypassed congressmen discussed in the preceding section who possessed advanced congressional seniority but who received no top committee post. Of the five bypassed Democratic Senators—Holland, Long, Stennis, Robertson, and Sparkman—the first three had changed committee. Robertson and Sparkman had the misfortune—assuming the chairmanship of the Senate Banking and Currency Committee is good fortune—of being appointed to that committee, where another senior Southerner, J. W. Fulbright, out-ranked them. Of the fifteen top-ranking bypassed Democratic Representatives in 1957–58, only three had switched committees. Another seven were initially appointed to Ways and Means or Appropriations, where they could expect to be outranked for some time to come, but where other benefits could be expected from serving on two such powerful committees. However, the other five were appointed to committees such as Banking and Currency, Agriculture, and Armed Services and found themselves out-ranked by more senior members.

Summary

THE FINDINGS CLEARLY WARN AGAINST THE DANGER of letting the congressional party define the operation or effects of the seniority system. The average congressional seniority required to gain top committee rank varies considerably from Senate to House and from Republicans to Democrats. Senators, in fact, need win on the average only two elections to qualify for leadership. Further, by far the greatest number of committee leaders stay a relatively short time in their posts. The median number ranges between five and ten years, with a substantial proportion serving only four years or less. In light of these facts, critics who remark on the fact that chairmen were first elected "a generation ago" need to specify whether they refer to a Senate or House generation, a Democratic or Republican generation. "Seniority" as a concept implying time varies with the party and the house of Congress under discussion.

Second, committee leaders are not so distinctive a breed in advanced congressional service as to preclude a majority of congressmen from a chance at chairmanships. The congressional seniority requirement presupposed by the seniority system does not appear sufficiently restrictive to screen out of the selection process more than a fairly small minority of states and districts. Thus the traditional argument that the system benefits only the safest states and districts may have to be reversed to read that the system penalizes only the most competitive—a reversal in emphasis of considerable importance.

Third, while length of congressional service does influence who becomes a committee leader, a number of exceptions can be noted. Some can be explained by the separate influence of the committee seniority requirement, others merely by the luck or discretion involved in the initial committee assignment. These facts together point to the possibility that sheer length of service in Congress may be less crucial a determinant of committee leadership than many have supposed.

III

Constituencies: by Geography

O<small>NE OF THE MORE FREQUENT CRITICISMS</small> leveled against the seniority system is that it produces chairmen geographically unrepresentative of their party in Congress. Such alleged built-in unrepresentativeness is of considerable interest in a nation where sectional interests are still strong, often conflicting with other interests and goals, and where sectional loyalties and mutual distrust run deep. That there has been for some time a "Southern" view on certain questions needs no belaboring. "Western" issues can also be identified, centering on the politics of water and public works. Whereas Southern views have been set by history and the strains of Southern society, Western politics has been largely formed by the problems of physical environment. The scarcity of water and the necessity to rely on the federal government as the major source of capital for ambitious projects of land (and water) development have made federal reclamation projects, public power regulation, and rivers and harbors serious Western political business.[1] There may not be so clearly identifiable "Midwestern" or "Eastern" issues, since these regions have a less homogeneous set of problems, but views of Midwestern and Eastern congressmen will often conflict with the views of their colleagues to the South and West and also conflict with each other.[2] And certainly, if we consider not large regions but states or small groups of states, it is obvious that further interests can be identified—for example, the politics of oil or of the St. Lawrence Seaway project.

The point should not be carried too far. Geography has only limited utility for explaining the policy stands taken in Congress. But it does have some. Congress mirrors the interests of diverse sections and states—interests which are, to some extent, defined by geography. It is of considerable interest to determine to what extent the seniority system benefits some regions over others by elevating their representatives to the top committee posts.

The four major regions of the country—East, South, Midwest, and West—have been employed in traditional discussions of the subject and will be utilized for the first investigation here.[3] This will be followed by a state-by-state analysis which brings out points that regional classifications obscure. Both regional and state-by-state analyses will attempt (1) to trace patterns of representativeness, committee leaders compared to members of Congress; and (2) to specify the extent to which the seniority system—in particular, the congressional seniority requirement—has been instrumental in forming these patterns.

Representation by Region: Leadership and Membership

COMPARISON OF COMMITTEE LEADERS AND ALL members for the full twenty-year span, by party and house of Congress, may reveal some surprises. The results are presented in Table 6. To turn to the Senate first, it is clear from the table that in general, for both Democrats and Republicans, the region with the largest number of members of Congress has the largest number of committee posts, and so on. Measured in terms of overall unrepresentativeness (summing the differences between frequencies in those cases where chairmen exceed members), Democratic chairmen exhibit a less close fit than Republicans, with an index number of overall unrepresentativeness of 23, compared to the Republican index of 10.[4] It may be surprising to note that *two* regions are overrepresented in the Democratic Party: not only the South, but the West as well.

36

TABLE 6.   REGIONAL REPRESENTATION: COMMITTEE CHAIRMEN
AND RANKING MINORITY MEMBERS COMPARED TO ALL MEMBERS,
1947–1966[a]

	DEMOCRATS		REPUBLICANS	
REGION	% of All Members	% of CC's/ RMM's	% of All Members	% of CC's/ RMM's
Senate				
East	18	10	38	39
South	42	53	2	1
Midwest	17	3	37	46
West	23	35	23	13
Total	99	101	100	99
House				
East	25	19	36	35
South	45	61	5	1
Midwest	19	14	43	51
West	11	6	15	14
Total	100	100	99	101

a. All congressmen are counted once for each election won: Representatives, from 1946; Senators, from 1942. Only those congressmen elected at regular elections are included. Committee leaders are counted only for those elections which precede their terms in top committee posts. For example, Warren Magnuson served as chairman or ranking minority member of the Senate Commerce Committee from 1955 to 1966. He is thus counted, (or "Washington" or the "West" is thus counted) three times—on the basis of his reelection in 1950, 1956, and 1962.

This procedure permits a measurement of the complexion of membership and leadership over the full time-span. By contrast, a counting of individual congressmen (each man once no matter how long he served), by giving equal weight to Representatives of two or twenty years' service, would not provide as accurate an aggregate description.

The numbers of congressmen per election won on which these percentages are based are as follows: Members: SD, 226; SR, 159; HD, 2464; HR, 1885; Committee Leaders: SD, 72; SR, 69; HD, 194; HR, 190.

This Western overrepresentation merits further attention. While the West has its share of conservatives, too, a point to be developed in Chapter V, some of these Western chairmen are far removed on the political spectrum from their Southern chairmen-colleagues. Warren G. Magnuson of Washington, Chairman of the Senate Commerce Committee, and Henry M. Jackson, also of Washington, Chairman of the Interior Committee, would be considered "liberal" Democrats.[5] While Senator Clinton Anderson of New Mexico, Chairman of the Senate Committee on Aeronautics and Space, and past Chairman of

Interior, has a distinctly unliberal voting record, he was one of the leaders of the fight to change the cloture rule and a co-sponsor of Senator Joseph Clark's attempt to liberalize the Democratic Steering Committee by enlarging its membership.

Results for the House are similar: The Republican leadership seems less unrepresentative of its membership than that of the Democrats. The literature on the seniority system has not attempted to distinguish between House and Senate, Democratic and Republican parties. One of the few remarks addressed to the subject was Senator Joseph Clark's comment that geographic unrepresentativeness was to be found more clearly in the Senate than in the House.[6] Clark did not distinguish between parties. Yet the present evidence suggests a party difference and no Senate-House difference. Both Senate and House Democrats were less accurately represented in the committee leadership than Senate and House Republicans.

Perhaps the main point to stress from this preliminary analysis is that much of the Southern "overrepresentation" so widely noted is merely a matter of numbers. The South predominates in the membership of the congressional Democratic party. If more than 50 per cent of the committee leaders are from the South, this is because, as a result of congressional elections over the past twenty years, nearly 50 per cent of the Democratic party membership in both Senate and House has been from the South. In this situation, even a choice of committee leaders by lot would be expected to produce the same results.

For example, suppose the chairmen were selected by alphabetical order of last names, rather than by seniority. In three out of four Congresses examined, approximately as many Southern Democratic Senators would have been committee leaders under a selection by alphabetical order as under a selection by seniority. The results are given in Table 7.

These findings do not appear to mask regional differences in the prestige of the committees which the chairmen head. Admittedly, only limited evidence is available. Using the Miller-Stokes six-level ranking of House committees by prestige,

TABLE 7. SENATE DEMOCRATIC COMMITTEE LEADERS AS SELECTED
BY THE SENIORITY SYSTEM AND BY ALPHABETICAL ORDER[a]

	NUMBER OF COMMITTEE LEADERS							
	1947–48		1955–56		1961–62		1963–64	
REGION	Senior-ity	Alpha-bet	Senior-ity	Alpha-bet	Senior-ity	Alpha-bet	Senior-ity	Alpha-bet
East	2	2	3	1	0	1	0	2
South	7	8	8	9	10	8	10	5
Midwest	0	0	0	2	0	4	1	6
West	6	5	4	3	6	3	5	3
Total	15	15	15	15	16	16	16	16

a. The "selection" by alphabetical order was made by arranging the last names of the full Senate Democratic membership in alphabetical order and designating every third or fourth one, depending on membership size in the particular Congress, as hypothetical chairman.

it appears that the Democratic chairmen are distributed fairly evenly across the range of committee rankings. The results are presented in Table 8. While committees ranked highest in prestige had a slightly higher proportion of Southern chairmen than some other rankings, the committees ranked *lowest* in prestige were headed only by Southern members. Republican committee leaders also showed no regional variation by prestige ranking of committee; Midwestern and Eastern committee leaders were distributed evenly throughout the ranking and Western committee leaders were found on rank I, III, and V committees.

If we extend the time span beyond the 1947–66 period, we find that in the 1920's (from the 1920 election through the 1930 election), Southern Democrats composed 55 per cent of Senate membership and 78 per cent of the committee leadership, 63 per cent of House membership and 83 per cent of the committee leadership on the committees considered most important during that decade. Since then, the proportion of Southerners has been declining, although erratically. This contradicts the suggestion made by Raymond Wolfinger and Joan Heifetz that the widespread defeat of Northern Democrats in the 1946 election led to an increased Southern predominance in committee leadership.[7] On the contrary, the decade following the 1946 election marked the lowest point in four decades of South-

TABLE 8. REGIONAL DISTRIBUTION OF CHAIRMEN BY COMMITTEE "PRESTIGE"[a] HOUSE DEMOCRATS, 1947–1966.

Committees by Prestige (High to Low)	All CC's No.	Southern No.	(%)	Eastern No.	(%)	Midwestern No.	(%)	Western No.	(%)
I Rules									
Ways & Means	7	5	(71)	0	(0)	2	(29)	0	(0)
Approp.									
II Foreign Affairs									
Armed Services	7	3	(43)	3	(43)	1	(14)	0	(0)
III Judiciary									
Commerce	7	4	(57)	1	(14)	1	(14)	1	(14)
Agriculture									
IV Science									
Education	10	5	(50)	3	(30)	1	(10)	1	(10)
Public Works									
Banking									
V Gov. Op.									
House Adm.									
Dist. of Col.	14	7	(50)	3	(21)	1	(7)	3	(21)
Interior									
Merchant Mar.									
VI Post Office	3	3	(100)	0	(0)	0	(0)	0	(0)
Veterans									

a. Based on the Miller-Stokes six-level ranking of committees by prestige. See Warren E. Miller and Donald E. Stokes, *Representation in the American Congress*, forthcoming.

ern predominance, as the figures in Table 9 show. In fact, Southern Senators were slightly "underrepresented" after 1946, receiving 52 per cent of the Senate seats but only 48 per cent of the committee posts—if this can be called underrepresentation.

In general, the election results of the past twenty years have worked to reduce regional concentration within parties. Among both House and Senate Democrats, the South has lost some of its relative predominance, while the other three regions have increased their number of Democratic congressmen. The Republican change has not been as large, but the South has gained some Republican Senators; both South and West have gained in relative proportions of House membership. All of these changes tend toward more even representation of the major regions in the membership of Congress. If these trends continue, we may

TABLE 9. REGIONAL REPRESENTATION IN THE DEMOCRATIC PARTY FOR FOUR DECADES: COMMITTEE CHAIRMEN AND RANKING MINORITY MEMBERS COMPARED TO ALL MEMBERS[a]

REGION		*1921–32*		*1933–46*		*1947–56*		*1957–66*	
		% of All Members	% of CC's/ RMM's	% of All Members	% of CC's/ RMM's	% of All Members	% of CC's/ RMM's	% of All Members	% of CC's/ RMM's
SENATE	N	(90)	(23)	(158)	(41)	(117)	(40)	(143)	(40)
East		14	0	20	15	17	17	18	5
South		55	78	40	59	52	48	35	57
Midwest		9	4	15	2	10	0	22	5
West		21	17	26	24	22	35	25	33
Total		99	99	101	100	101	100	100	100
HOUSE	N	(1,070)	(66)	(1,859)	(77)	(1,131)	(95)	(1,324)	(99)
East		19	8	25	9	24	18	26	20
South		63	83	44	72	51	60	41	62
Midwest		14	0	21	10	17	18	21	10
West		4	9	10	9	9	4	13	8
Total		100	101	100	100	101	100	101	100

a. Each Senator and Representative is counted once for each election won in the decade. Committee leadership before 1947 is based on the heads of eleven major Senate and twelve major House committees.

expect to see them reflected in committee leadership, with some delay because of the time lag due to the seniority system. Some glimpse of the future trend can be gained from looking at the second and third ranking committee members in each party during the 89th Congress (1965–66), since these men are already high enough on the seniority ladder to have demonstrated electoral durability. When the regional distribution of these members is compared with the 1957–66 distribution

TABLE 10. Possible Future Trends: Comparison of Committeee Leaders of 1957-66 with the Second and Third Ranking Members of 1965-66

Region	% of CC's/RMM's 1957–66	% of Second and Third Ranking Members 1965–66
Senate Democrats	(N = 40)	(N = 32)
East	5	13
South	57	47
Midwest	5	9
West	33	31
Total	100	100
House Democrats	(N = 99)	(N = 40)
East	20	20
South	62	55
Midwest	10	18
West	8	8
Total	100	100
Senate Republicans	(N = 37)	(N = 32)
East	46	26
South	3	19
Midwest	35	29
West	16	26
Total	100	100
House Republicans	(N = 95)	(N = 40)
East	38	25
South	1	13
Midwest	52	45
West	9	18
Total	100	101

42

(Table 10), one can see in all four groups a smoothing out of regional inequalities. The four regions within each group are similar in seniority proportions.

One comment can be added. Differences between majority and minority parties cannot explain the interparty differences in regional representation. The Democratic committee leaders were as unrepresentative in the Senate when they were the minority party in the 1920's as when they were the majority party in 1947–1966; and in the House they seemed even more unrepresentative in the 1920's. The Republicans exhibited approximately the same degree of representativeness as majority party in the 1920's as they did as minority party more recently.[8] The interparty difference has remained the same over time, whichever party controlled Congress.

The Impact of Congressional Seniority

ALTHOUGH MUCH OF THE SOUTHERN CAST TO DEMO-cratic committee leadership was not due to overrepresentation, but merely reflected the Southern predominance in congressional membership, some overrepresentation did exist— most notably among Southern and Western Democrats and Midwestern Republicans. To what extent is this overrepresentation a result of the congressional seniority requirement? Does this requirement screen out enough members so that the distribution of senior members is different from the distribution for all members and similar to the distribution for committee leaders? What difference would it make if congressmen of low seniority had an even chance of becoming committee leaders?

Table 11, covering the full time span, repeats the distributions for committee leaders and members as presented in Table 6 and adds the distribution for all congressional "seniors" serving during the same period. If seniority provides a redistributive effect, one would expect that (1) the percentages for seniors would be closer to the percentages for committee lead-

TABLE 11. MEMBERS, SENIORS, AND COMMITTEE LEADERS
BY REGION, 1947–1966[a]

REGION	% of Members	% of Seniors	% of CC's/ RMM's	% of Members	% of Seniors	% of CC's/ RMM's
	Senate Democrats			House Democrats		
East	18	9	10	25	20	19
South	42	58	53	45	63	61
Midwest	17	8	3	19	12	14
West	23	26	35	11	5	6
Total	99	101	101	100	100	100
	Senate Republicans			House Republicans		
East	38	39	39	36	36	35
South	2	1	1	5	1	1
Midwest	37	42	46	43	53	51
West	23	18	13	15	10	14
Total	100	100	99	99	100	101

a. Members, seniors, and committee leaders are each counted once each time elected, for each election preceding their term in that classification (e.g., as "senior" or as chairman). For full explanation, see page 60. Numbers for seniors, not previously given, are Senate Democrats, N = 113; House Democrats, N = 398; Senate Republicans, N = 84; and House Republicans, N = 418.

ers than to those for members (or as close to them), or at least that (2) they would be closer to the percentages for committee leaders than the latter are to the percentages for members.

The results indicate that some such redistribution has occurred. In fourteen of sixteen cases, the percentage for seniors is closer to the percentage for committee leaders than it is to that for members. In all cases the percentage for leaders is closer to that for seniors than to that for members. Focusing on the clearest cases of overrepresentation, one can see that the relatively high proportions of seniors among Southern Democrats and Midwestern Republicans are quite similar to the proportions of their committee leaders. But this phenomenon is not so obviously true in the case of Western Senators.

A closer examination of Democratic party patterns for one Congress can clarify the point. The 88th Congress (1963–64) has been selected to give maximum play to the congressional seniority variable. By 1963 the South had lost its predominant

44

position in the Democratic party. Both Midwestern and Eastern states had been gaining Democrats for a decade but presumably their congressmen would be too new in membership to have earned substantial amounts of congressional seniority. Table 12 presents the regional distribution for members, sen-

TABLE 12.   MEMBERS, SENIORS, COMMITTEE SENIORS, AND CHAIRMEN BY REGION: DEMOCRATS, 1963–64[a]

REGION		% of Members	% of Seniors	% of Advanced Seniors	% of Committee Seniors	% of Chairmen
		SENATE				
	N	(64)	(25)	(23)	(15)	(16)
East		19	4	0	0	0
South		36	64	74	67	63
Midwest		23	12	9	7	6
West		22	20	17	27	31
Total		100	100	100	101	100
		HOUSE				
	N	(255)	(67)	(51)	(44)	(20)
East		25	21	21	20	20
South		41	60	59	64	60
Midwest		18	13	12	11	10
West		15	6	8	5	10
Total		99	100	100	100	100

a. Although the percentages are based on small numbers, their use seems advisable in this case to describe changing patterns of advantage across the table. For definition of "senior" and "advanced senior" see page 25.

iors,[9] committee seniors,[10] and chairmen. Numbers given at the heading of each column should help describe the narrowing process of selection.

Reading across the table for the Southern frequencies in both Senate and House, it seems clear that the crucial change in percentage occurs between columns 1 and 2—membership and congressional seniority. Althouh the South composed only 36 per cent of the Senate Democratic membership by the 88th Congress, it had 64 per cent of the seniors and 63 per cent of the committee chairs. For the South, the redistribution is clear, and the change in proportions of senior members seems capable of explaining it.

It is not so clear, however, for the West. With 22 per cent of the Senate Democratic membership, the West had only 20 per cent of the seniors and 17 per cent of the more advanced seniors—a slight penalty rather than an advantage received by the seniority requirement. But the Western states captured 31 per cent of the chairs. Inspection suggests that patterns of committee seniority or of original committee assignments gave the West its disproportionate share of posts. The relative advantage can be explained in another way. By 1962 twenty-five members had served sufficiently long in the Senate to be likely candidates for a chairmanship. With only sixteen chairs available, some of these Senators had to be bypassed, and it might be expected that some from each region would be bypassed. But in this particular game of musical chairs, the West, with five seniors, had five chairmen.

Of the five Western chairmen, four were seniors: Jackson of Washington, Anderson of New Mexico, Hayden of Arizona, and Magnuson of Washington. The fifth senior nonchairman could not really be called "bypassed" either, since he was the Senate Majority Leader—Mansfield of Montana. One nonsenior Westerner was also a chairman—Bible of Nevada.

State-by-State Representation

IF THE MAKE-UP OF CONGRESS IS AS IMPORTANT AN influence on committee leadership as the preceding results suggest, then one would expect that a state-by-state analysis would show even clearer evidence of this than the preceding regional analysis. The Senate membership is elected by states and the House by districts allotted on the basis of state population. The regional categories utilized above and used in all the standard discussions of the subject may be merely artificial constructs combining and possibly obscuring the state-by-state results.

This final section concentrates on the relative contribution of a state's total congressional membership and the congressional seniority of its members in determining committee leadership. A state-by-state breakdown presented in Tables 13 and 14 and correlation analysis should clarify the relative influence of both factors.

"Membership" is taken to refer to the number of congressional party members a state has elected over time. This index should not be read merely as measuring a state's electoral safeness. Election results over time do provide a measure for safeness, but they also determine the membership of the Congress. This truism is made explicit to focus attention on the influence of the sheer weight of *numbers* in a congressional party in determining the distribution of committee leadership. If committee leadership selection is a kind of lottery, the more members in a congressional party from a given state, the more committee leaders that state can be expected to receive.

The importance of numerical strength in congressional party membership—the "lottery" aspect of the seniority system—is vividly shown in Table 13. This table reports for the Senate,

TABLE 13. MEMBERS, SENIORS, AND COMMITTEE LEADERS BY STATE: SENATE, 1947–1966

	DEMOCRATS			REPUBLICANS		
	Senators Elected No.	Seniors No.	CC's/ RMM's No.	Senators Elected No.	Seniors No.	CC's/ RMM's No.
Alabama	6	2	1	0	0	0
Arkansas	6	2	2	0	0	0
Georgia	6	3	2	0	0	0
Florida	6	3	0	0	0	0
Louisiana	6	3	2	0	0	0
Mississippi	6	3	1	0	0	0
New Mexico	6	3	3	0	0	0
N. Carolina	6	2	1	0	0	0
Oklahoma	6	2	3	0	0	0
Rhode Island	6	2	2	0	0	0
S. Carolina	6	2	2	0	0	0
Tennessee	6	2	1	0	0	0

TABLE 13.—*cont.*

	DEMOCRATS			REPUBLICANS		
	Senators Elected No.	*Seniors No.*	*CC's/ RMM's No.*	*Senators Elected No.*	*Seniors No.*	*CC's/ RMM's No.*
Texas	6	2	2	0	0	0
Virginia	6	2	2	0	0	0
Missouri	5	2	1	1	0	0
Montana	5	2	2	1	0	0
Washington	5	2	2	1	0	1
W. Virginia	5	2	2	1	0	1
Arizona	4	2	1	2	1	1
Minnesota	4	1	0	2	1	0
Nevada	4	2	2	2	1	1
Oregon	4	0	0	2	1	0
Wyoming	4	1	1	2	0	0
Connecticut	3	0	0	3	0	0
Idaho	3	1	0	3	1	1
Illinois	3	2	0	3	1	2
Kentucky	3	0	0	3	1	1
Michigan	3	1	1	3	2	1
Ohio	3	0	0	3	2	2
Colorado	2	1	1	4	2	1
Delaware	2	1	0	4	1	3
Indiana	2	0	0	4	2	2
Maryland	2	1	1	4	2	2
Massachusetts	2	1	0	4	1	2
Pennsylvania	2	0	0	4	2	1
S. Dakota	2	0	0	4	2	2
Wisconsin	2	0	0	4	2	3
California	1	0	0	5	2	1
Iowa	1	0	0	5	2	1
Maine	1	0	0	5	2	2
New Jersey	1	0	0	5	2	1
New York	1	0	1	5	2	1
Utah	1	0	1	5	2	1
Kansas	0	0	0	6	2	3
Nebraska	0	0	0	6	4	3
New Hampshire	0	0	0	6	3	3
N. Dakota	0	0	0	6	2	1
Vermont	0	0	0	6	3	2
Total	164	55	40	124	51	46

48

by state, the number of congressional party members elected from 1946 through the 1962 election,[11] the number of individual seniors, and the number of individual committee leaders. Comparing the first and third columns for both parties, one can see how strong a relationship there is between the number of Democrats or Republicans elected from the state and the number of Democratic or Republican committee leaders from the state. The correlation coefficients between members and committee leaders are high for both parties: for Senate Democrats, $r = .72$; for Senate Republicans, $r = .77$. Squaring the two correlation coefficients yields coefficients of determination of .52 and .59, respectively, indicating that 52 per cent and 59 per cent of the variation in committee leadership can be statistically explained by the variation in membership.

Congressional seniority exerts only a small influence beyond that of membership. For Senate Democrats, the number of members elected by a state accounts for 52 per cent of the variation, while a multiple correlation analysis using number of members and number of seniors shows that these variables together account for 56 per cent of the variation. For Senate Republicans, membership accounts for 59 per cent of the variation, while membership plus seniority accounts for 62 per cent. The relatively small independent effect[12] of congressional seniority is understandable in terms of the point made earlier— that the congressional tenure requirement is not as restrictive as is sometimes supposed. Forty of the forty-eight states managed to produce at least two seniors from the same party. Eight states produced three.

In a similar analysis of the House, a complicating factor must be considered. The size of a state's House delegation depends on its population, while all states have equal representation in the Senate. We can control for this factor statistically. When we do so, the partial correlation between members and committee leaders for House Democrats is .71; for House Republicans, .73—extremely similar to the Senate correlations of .72 and .77, respectively.[13]

49

If one simply relates number of Representatives elected and number of committee leaders, as presented in Table 14, one

TABLE 14. MEMBERS, SENIORS, AND COMMITTEE LEADERS, BY
STATE: HOUSE OF REPRESENTATIVES, 1947–1966

	DEMOCRATS				REPUBLICANS		
	Representatives Elected No.	Seniors No.	CC's RMM's No.		Representatives Elected No.	Seniors No.	CC's RMM's No.
Texas	213	15	4	New York	229	26	8
New York	201	13	5	Pennsylvania	173	10	6
California	144	7	3	Ohio	157	15	9
Pennsylvania	130	6	2	California	151	18	6
Illinois	113	5	3	Illinois	140	10	9
N. Carolina	109	7	4	Michigan	114	11	7
Georgia	99	5	2	New Jersey	86	11	8
Missouri	87	4	1	Indiana	73	5	1
Alabama	83	8	1	Wisconsin	72	7	1
Virginia	82	8	4	Massachusetts	69	9	3
Louisiana	80	6	2	Iowa	64	8	4
Florida	74	3	1	Kansas	52	3	2
Ohio	73	3	1	Minnesota	50	5	2
Tennessee	71	5	3	Washington	50	5	1
Massachusetts	67	4	0	Nebraska	34	3	1
Michigan	65	2	1	Connecticut	32	2	0
Kentucky	63	6	1	Missouri	27	1	1
Mississippi	60	7	2	Oregon	25	3	0
S. Carolina	60	3	3	Maine	24	3	0
Arkansas	59	5	2	Maryland	22	1	0
Oklahoma	55	3	0	Tennessee	22	0	0
Maryland	47	2	1	New Hampshire	19	1	0
West Virginia	47	3	1	Kentucky	18	0	0
Minnesota	38	1	0	N. Dakota	18	0	0
Indiana	37	2	0	S. Dakota	18	2	0
Connecticut	28	0	0	Colorado	17	1	1
Wisconsin	28	1	0	Virginia	15	2	0
Colorado	23	2	1	Oklahoma	11	1	0
New Jersey	20	2	2	Utah	11	0	0
New Mexico	20	0	0	W. Virginia	11	0	0
Rhode Island	20	0	0	Idaho	10	0	0
Washington	17	0	0	N. Carolina	9	0	0
Arizona	15	1	1	Vermont	9	1	0
Oregon	15	0	0	Wyoming	9	0	0
Iowa	14	0	0	Florida	8	1	1
Montana	12	0	0	Montana	8	0	0
Idaho	10	0	0	Arizona	7	1	0
Utah	9	0	0	Texas	6	0	0
Nevada	7	0	0	Alabama	5	0	0
Kansas	6	0	0	Delaware	5	0	0
Delaware	5	0	0	Nevada	3	0	0
Maine	4	0	0	Georgia	1	0	0
Nebraska	4	0	0	Mississippi	1	0	0
N. Dakota	2	0	0	Arkansas	0	0	0
S. Dakota	2	0	0	Louisiana	0	0	0
New Hampshire	1	0	0	New Mexico	0	0	0
Vermont	1	0	0	Rhode Island	0	0	0
Wyoming	1	0	0	S. Carolina	0	0	0
Total	2,401	139	51	Total	1,885	166	71

finds an extremely strong relationship on a state-by-state basis: Democrats, $r = .83$; Republicans, $r = .91$. Membership alone statistically explains 69 per cent and 83 per cent of the variations in outcome for the two congressional parties. Congressional seniority adds a separate, although small, increment, raising the percentages to 75 and 84, respectively. Use of the stricter definition for congressional seniority for both House and Senate produced no significantly different results. The correlations betwen seniority and committee leadership for Senate Democrats and House Republicans were slightly higher; for Senate Republicans, slightly lower; and for House Democrats, the same.[14]

At this point one can see what regional classifications obscure. Eight states (spread over the four regions) produced three or more Democratic chairmen, and six of the eight were in the top quartile of Democrats elected. Thus New York, second only to Texas in number of Democrats elected, produced the largest number of Democratic chairmen—five. For the Republicans, seven states (spread over three of the four regions) produced six or more committee leaders, the same top seven states in number of Republicans elected. Considering the states heading both Democratic and Republican lists—New York, California, Illinois, and Pennsylvania—the process of selection in the House would appear to favor the same states for chairmen as the electoral college does for the presidency.[15]

The House results, strikingly similar to those for the Senate, show the underlying correspondence between membership and leadership and suggest that discussions of "bias" in the committee chairs may overlook the fact that congressional party membership itself is "biased" if one means simply that a small proportion of states supply over time a large proportion of the party's membership to House and Senate; that, for example, as regards House Democrats, Northern urban and Southern rural districts have supplied the bulk of that congressional party's membership in the past twenty years and the bulk of the party's committee chairmen.

Summary

MUCH OF THE "OVERREPRESENTATION" CITED IN criticisms of the seniority system is not overrepresentation at all; the number of committee leaders from a given state or region is roughly proportional to the size of its delegation in Congress. Committee leaders may represent areas of traditional party strength not so much because the seniority rule favors them as because those areas electing over time the largest number of congressmen will stand the best chance of gaining committee posts. The congressional seniority requirement does have one important effect, which consists not in systematically restricting the number of congressmen qualifying for leadership, but simply in building a *time lag* into the process of representation after periods of partisan realignment. When the character of a congressional party begins to change—for example, when the Democratic party becomes less overwhelmingly Southern and begins to gain more Midwestern or Eastern members—it takes some time before this change is reflected in the chairmanships. Only in the late 1960's did the Democratic leadership begin to show the effects of the election results of the past ten years.

Within the basic limits set by the number of members in a congressional party, congressional seniority does exert a separate "redistributive" effect, although the case of Western overrepresentation suggests a point to be explored more fully in the following two chapters—that factors relating to patterns of committee assignment may also influence the results.

IV

Constituencies: by Population Type

Is THERE, as some critics have charged, a population bias built into the seniority system, which in the House favors rural districts for the chairmanships at the expense of urban districts, and in the Senate correspondingly favors states of small population at the expense of states of large population, the latter including the major metropolitan centers of the country?

Most people would accept the view that the presidency has been more accessible and sympathetic than the Congress to the urban, large-state interests of the nation, and that the Congress has been admirably suited for protecting such "minorities in retreat" as Southern segregationist and rural constituencies by its system of plural leadership and multiple points of veto built into the legislative process. The question posed in this chapter is the extent to which the seniority system reinforces this tendency already present in Congress, by giving further advantage to rural districts and the less populous states.

The growing involvement of the national government with explosive urban problems, and the growing realization that large segments of rural and urban America do not understand each other, lend significance to this particular charge concerning the seniority system. It is true that patterns of accommodation seem to have been worked out in the Democratic party during the past two decades whereby rural congressmen support city issues in return for urban congressmen's support of

53

farm programs. Thus, urban Chairman Adolph Sabath of Illinois can be found supporting in floor debate such Western rural concerns as a mineral subsidy bill.[1] Such reciprocal generosity may have helped, in the past at least, to soften the sharpest edges of the rural-urban division. These patterns of accommodation, however, did not extend to the Republican party. And even among Democrats, Southern rural congressmen were noticeably less generous in supporting Northern urban issues than they were in supporting Northern rural issues, such as Midwestern farm programs. For example, it has been a common occurrence to find Southern rural Democrats offering crippling amendments to such Democratic party programs as housing legislation.[2] And since the rural overrepresentation of chairmen referred to by the critics is essentially a *Southern* rural overrepresentation, the distribution of committee posts may well have considerable political consequences.

Leadership and Membership: States by Population

SENATE AND HOUSE COMPARISONS ARE DIFFICULT in this case because measures of ruralism and urbanism cannot usually describe the state as a whole. However, an analysis for the Senate can be carried out by using population as a measure. Admittedly imprecise, it can at least serve to distinguish between states of largest and smallest population, and the interesting questions concern the states at both extremes. Are the "small" states of the nation benefited in the Senate committee leadership at the expense of the large, urban states? Given the strong correlations found between state-by-state membership and committee leaders, one would expect to find no particular bias, unless the states most consistent in their party attachments were also similar in population.

The findings as reported in Table 15 support this negative expectation. States are arranged in quartiles by population according to the 1960 census and compared for the distribution of

TABLE 15. SENATE COMMITTEE LEADERS COMPARED TO ALL SENATORS, 1957–66, FROM STATES ARRANGED BY POPULATION, 1960 CENSUS[a]

STATES BY POPULATION	DEMOCRATS		REPUBLICANS	
	% of All Senators ($N=143$)	*% of CC's/ RMM's* ($N=40$)	*% of All Senators* ($N=82$)	*% of CC's/ RMM's* ($N=37$)
1st Quartile[b]	27	7	25	30
2nd Quartile	28	40	17	16
3rd Quartile	25	32	23	19
4th Quartile	20	20	35	35
Total	100	99	100	100

Source: U.S. Bureau of the Census, *Congressional District Data Book:* A Statistical Abstract Supplement (Washington, D.C.: Government Printing Office, 1963).
   a. Each Senator is counted once each time elected. First quartile states include California, Florida, Illinois, Indiana, Massachusetts, Michigan, New Jersey, New York, North Carolina, Ohio, Pennsylvania, Texas. Second quartile states: Alabama, Georgia, Iowa, Kentucky, Louisiana, Maryland, Minnesota, Missouri, Tennessee, Virginia, Washington, Wisconsin. Third quartile states: Arizona, Arkansas, Colorado, Connecticut, Kansas, Maine, Mississippi, Nebraska, Oklahoma, Oregon, South Carolina, West Virginia. Fourth quartile states: Delaware, Idaho, Montana, Nevada, New Hampshire, New Mexico, North Dakota, Rhode Island, South Dakota, Utah, Vermont, Wyoming.
   b. States of largest population.

committee leaders and members serving within the decade from 1957 to 1966. States of largest population are underrepresented among the committee leadership in the Democratic party and very slightly overrepresented in the Republican party. States of smallest population are equitably represented in both parties. Indeed, the Republican party distributions show no significant difference in percentages of leaders to members.[3] The Democratic overrepresentation of second-quartile states may well be reducible to the Southern overrepresentation already discussed, since six of the twelve second-quartile states are Southern.[4] In the Senate, at least, no clear population bias is apparent.

Leadership and Membership: Rural and Urban Districts

TO WHAT EXTENT IS COMMITTEE LEADERSHIP BIased in the House by the population type, rural or urban, of district represented? This charge is more difficult to test than some of the others. Widespread changes in congressional district boundaries, resulting from the past two censuses and the impact of *Westberry v. Sanders,* have affected the "rural" and "urban" character of districts over time, making it difficult to characterize congressmen's districts for any considerable portion of the twenty years being studied. The *Congressional Quarterly* has undertaken a demographic analysis of congressional districts three times and has used each time a different classification scheme.[5] Yet the *Congressional Quarterly* analyses are more discriminating than a simple urban-rural dichotomy, and it is of interest to ascertain whether any *consistent* population bias holds across the full range of congressional districts or whether it affects merely one or the other of these two demographic extremes. The first of the three *CQ* classifications—for 1955–56—was found the most useful for this analysis: a division of congressional districts into four categories: rural, small-town, midurban, and metropolitan.[6] A modification of *CQ*'s 1963–64 classification can be used to gain results roughly comparable with the 1955–56 scheme.[7] This particular inquiry, then, is based on alignments in the 1955–56 and 1963–64 Congresses only, and interpretation is more tentative because of that limitation.

Table 16 presents the results for the 1955–56 session. Since percentages may be misleading when based on such small numbers as the nineteen Democrats and nineteen Republicans who held the top committee positions at the time, two additional columns have been added to the standard percentage comparison. A third column, labeled "actual" distribution, gives the actual number of committee leaders, and a fourth column, labeled "expected" distribution, gives the number of committee leaders one could expect in each category based on the percentage of congressional membership in that category.

More than half of the Democratic chairmanships were held by congressmen from rural districts. The rural districts were

TABLE 16. DEMOGRAPHIC REPRESENTATION: HOUSE COMMITTEE CHAIRMEN AND RANKING MINORITY MEMBERS COMPARED TO ALL REPRESENTATIVES, 1955–56

CATEGORY	% of CC's/ RMM's	% of All Representatives	Actual No. of CC's/ RMM's	Expected No. of CC's/ RMM's
		DEMOCRATS		
Rural	58	26	11	5
Small-town	11	20	2	4
Midurban	16	17	3	3
Metropolitan	16	37	3	7
Total	101	100	19	19
		REPUBLICANS		
Rural	11	13	2	2
Small-town	47	31	9	6
Midurban	32	28	6	5
Metropolitan	11	28	2	5
Total	101	100	19	18

clearly overrepresented and the metropolitan districts clearly underrepresented among the 1955–56 House Democrats. Where, under an ideally representative system, one would expect five rural committee chairmen, one finds instead eleven. Where one would expect seven metropolitan chairmen, one finds only three. An interesting subsidiary finding is that the Democratic chairmen underrepresented their small-town district membership as well as their metropolitan district membership. No consistent population bias holds; bias appears to be concentrated in rural districts.

The Republican pattern, however, is markedly different. Republican ranking minority members for 1955–56 did not overrepresent rural districts. On the contrary, these districts were slightly underrepresented. The Republican overrepresentation occurred in the small-town and midurban categories. Republicans also underrepresented metropolitan districts. The differences between the two Republican distributions, however, are noticeably smaller than the Democratic differences. Again, no significant difference between leadership and membership distributions is found for the Republicans.[8]

A similar situation is found for 1963–64, as shown in Table 17, although the classification scheme is different. Democrats

TABLE 17. DEMOGRAPHIC REPRESENTATION: HOUSE COMMITTEE CHAIRMEN AND RANKING MINORITY MEMBERS COMPARED TO ALL REPRESENTATIVES, 1963–64

Category	% of CC's/ RMM's	% of All Representatives	Actual No. of CC's/ RMM's	Expected No. of CC's/ RMM's
	DEMOCRATS			
Rural	50	25	10	5
Mixed urban	25	36	5	7
Suburban	5	7	1	1
Urban	20	32	4	6
Total	100	100	20	19
	REPUBLICANS			
Rural	16	22	3	4
Mixed urban	58	50	11	10
Suburban	16	18	3	3
Urban	11	11	2	2
Total	101	101	19	19

overrepresented rural districts at the expense of all other districts, not merely the metropolitan districts. Where one would expect five rural committee chairmen, based on the percentage of membership, one finds instead ten. The Republican distribution for committee chairmen closely parallels its House membership, as a comparison of the actual and expected distribution shows. Republicans slightly *underrepresented* rural districts and slightly overrepresented mixed-urban districts. The suburban districts in 1963–64 were quite equitably represented in both parties.

It would appear that the rural predominance in the Democratic party cannot be explained away by the South, although with only eight non-Southern committee chairmen in 1963–64, interpretation is hazardous. But based on the percentage distribution of all Northern House Democrats in 1963–64,[9] the expected distribution is rural, one chairman; mixed-urban, two; suburban, one; and urban, four. The actual distribution is rural, three; mixed-urban, none; suburban, one; and urban, four. Even Northern rural districts in the Democratic House emerge with a slight advantage.

The Impact of Congressional Seniority

To what extent is this phenomenon of rural overrepresentation attributable to the seniority system? In particular, to what extent can it be attributed to the congressional seniority requirement? It was seen earlier that the safest seats in the House Democratic party were found in both the South (predominantly rural) and the urban North. One might therefore expect that the congressional seniority requirement would *not* favor rural districts over urban. In the regional analysis, Western overrepresentation could not be satisfactorily explained by congressional seniority. Perhaps rural overrepresentation also is due to some other factor.

This question can be explored by comparing the political history of rural and urban districts represented by Democrats in the 87th Congress (1961–62). This involves 72 rural and 81 urban districts, omitting the other Democratic districts—110 in all—typed as suburban or mixed-urban. (The 87th Congress was chosen over the 88th, used in the preceding investigation, because the reapportionment that occurred before the 1962 election would have greatly complicated the task of tracing districts and their congressmen back through the preceding decade. The patterns of representation for the two Congresses are almost identical.) In 1961–62 urban Representatives outnumbered rural Representatives 81 to 72, but they received only four chairmanships. Rural Representatives received nine.

Do differences betwen rural and urban districts in electoral safeness or in the turnover of candidates permit the inference that the congressional seniority requirement can explain this difference in outcome? If not, are there differences in congressional career patterns of Representatives—a tendency toward "committee hopping" or a countertendency to stay on the committee of initial appointment—by which committee seniority could explain these outcomes?

Table 18 traces from left to right how these two requirements would have "disqualified" some of the 1961–62 Representatives from chairmanships in that Congress. The word is used in quotes since some nonseniors do become chairmen, as Chapter II pointed out. In columns 1 and 2, one can see how many of the 1961–62 districts would have been disqualified by the requirement of party safeness. Sixty-five of the urban 1961–62 Representatives and 60 of the rural Representatives came from districts voting consistently Democratic back through the 1952 Eisenhower landslide. Thus party *safeness* cannot explain rural overrepresentation because the urban districts still outnumber the rural districts by this classification. Comparing columns 2 and 3, one can see the effect of candidate turnover. Since urban districts are less likely to return the same candidate than rural districts, the urban numerical advantage is lost. Only 39 of the 81 urban Representatives in 1961–62 had been in the House since 1952, whereas 42 of the 72 rural Representatives would thus qualify. Yet this fact, while interesting, is not sufficient to account for the difference in outcomes. Forty-two rural Representatives with nine chairmen as opposed to 39 urban Representatives with four chairmen is still a case of rural overrepresentation. Nor does extending the requirements back through 1946 give further clarification. Comparing columns 3 and 4, one finds almost the same number of rural and urban Representatives—21 and 18, respectively—who had carried their districts for the Democratic party as far back as 1946 and who averaged the same congressional seniority. Yet nine of these 21 rural Representatives were chairmen, and only four

TABLE 18. THE SENIORITY SYSTEM'S IMPACT ON RURAL AND URBAN SHARES
OF COMMITTEE POSTS IN 1961–62

	Democratic CD's[a] 1961–62	Congressional Seniority			Com. Seniority	Committee Posts
		CD's Democratic since 1952	CD's with Same Candidate since 1952	CD's with Same Candidate since 1946	CD's with Representative on Same Committee since 1946	
Rural CD's	72	60	42	21	19	9
Urban CD's	81	65	39	18	14	4

a. Congressional districts.

of the 18 urban Representatives were chairmen. These results cannot support the inference that congressional seniority patterns account for rural overrepresentation.[10]

Concerning the impact of committee seniority, two separate points should be made. First, the rural advantage seems partly attributable to a greater tendency for rural Representatives to stay on the committee of initial assignment.[11] Four of the 18 urban Representatives changed committees between 1947 and 1961, against 2 of the 21 rural Representatives. As in the case of candidate turnover, the slightly higher rate of committee change among urban Representatives may help to explain their loss of advantage in chairmanships. But it cannot explain their decided disadvantage. None of these factors linked to the seniority system—even in combination—is sufficient to explain the rural predominance in chairmanships.

The gain in rural relative advantage appears most clearly between columns 5 and 6. Of 19 Democrats and 14 urban Democrats who held the same committee seniority, nine of the former (or 47 per cent) and only four of the latter (or 28 per cent) were chairmen. This point, in effect, may be considered outside the seniority system altogether. It was labeled in the introductory discussion an area of "discretion or luck" involving patterns of committee assignment. In comparison to their urban, similarly senior, colleagues who similarly did not change committees, more rural congressmen became chairmen. One can speculate that it is the committee assignment process, discretionary or random, rather than the seniority system which creates this rural relative advantage. On some committees one becomes a chairman when on other committees a similarly senior colleague does not. It may be luck. But luck which benefits one influential group in Congress is curious, to say the least. It may be discretion on the part of party leaders or other influential congressmen who could persuade certain committee members to leave the committee, permitting others to gain rank faster. In any case, the question requires an extensive tracing of patterns in congressional careers. Now that the subject has been disengaged from the assumption that it is the "safe-seat bias" which creates the rural bias, such further investigation should be possible.

This chapter yields little evidence to support the point that the seniority system creates a population bias in chairmanships. In the Senate, no such bias was evident. Nor was any consistent bias observable for House Republicans. For House Democrats, rural overrepresentation could not be traced to the congressional seniority requirement. In fact, the two requirements of length of congressional service and length of committee service were not sufficient even in combination to explain this phenomenon.

V

Policy

CRITICS CHARGE that the seniority system tends to elevate to leadership (1) the most conservative element in each party; (2) those most opposed to the party's programs; and (3) those in the President's party who are most opposed to presidential programs. It thus further weakens and disperses the centralizing force located in the presidency and the party leadership of Congress, forces already weakened by a system of selecting independent and plural leadership. All would admit that effect of decentralization. The question remains, however, to what extent do committee leaders "misrepresent" the policy stands of their congressional party members? And to the extent such misrepresentation occurs, to what extent is this affected by the congressional seniority requirement?

Since policy differences are far more difficult to pinpoint than constituency characteristics, this chapter offers two different kinds of evidence: evidence from roll-call votes in Congress, commonly taken as an indicator of policy stands; and more impressionistic evidence of the views and activities of chairmen in their congressional context.[1]

Support of Party and President—Liberalism and Conservatism

SUPPORT OF ONE'S PARTY, SUPPORT OF THE PRESIdent, and support of liberal or conservative policies can for most purposes be considered together. Support of party and President are clearly related. And since recent Presidents have represented the "liberal" or "moderate" wing of their parties, support of the President usually comes from the more liberal element in the party. In the Democratic party, the three positions have been closely related. By supporting the Fair Deal, New Frontier, and Great Society programs, a Democrat could usually support his party, support the President, and take a liberal stance.

In the Republican party, the relationship has been more variable. The moderate Republican Eisenhower caused most uneasiness among the conservative wing of his party. Conservatives such as Senators Curtis (Nebraska), Young (North Dakota), and Case (South Dakota) have been high on the lists of Republicans who voted most often in opposition to Eisenhower programs.[2] Curtis and Case, by the way, were chairmen. With the Republican party out of power, however, and with Republicans perhaps feeling more comfortable in the role of critic of the Administration, a clear negative correlation is evident between support of the party and liberalism.[3] Those staunchest supporters of the party, such as Senators Bourke Hickenlooper, Karl Mundt, and Carl Curtis, are conservatives. Liberals, such as Jacob Javits and Thomas Kuchel, in this party are the mavericks. The conservative Nixon Administration has continued this pattern. Support of party and President in the 91st Congress has come from the conservatives.

Because of the general tendency for the three dimensions to overlap, with yet some discrepancy possible, the following strategy has been adopted. Where differences exist, they will be noted. However, in the frequent cases of close similarity among the three dimensions, only one will be discussed in detail.

According to the critics, the seniority system elevates those congressmen least likely to support party programs. An earlier comparison of voting records of chairmen and ranking minority members with those of all party members found that the committee leaders' average score on support of the party is slightly lower, though by only approximately 4 or 5 percentage points.[4]

These averages, however, conceal some intriguing differences betwen parties, as Table 19 shows. Republican Senate committee leaders again behave much like other Republicans.. The two distributions are almost identical. (An index of misrepresentation, derived by summing the difference in frequencies in

TABLE 19. PARTY SUPPORT: SENATE COMMITTEE CHAIRMEN AND RANKING MINORITY MEMBERS COMPARED TO ALL SENATORS, 1955–66[a]

Party Support Score %	All Members %	CC's/RMM's %
SENATE DEMOCRATS		
	(N=285)	(N=75)
0– 19	1	3
20– 39	10	21
40– 59	18	23
60– 79	48	41
80–100	23	12
Total	100	101
SENATE NORTHERN DEMOCRATS[b]		
	(N=176)	(N=29)
0– 19	1	0
20– 39	3	3
40– 59	9	28
60– 79	57	52
80–100	31	17
Total	101	100
SENATE REPUBLICANS		
	(N=190)	(N=72)
0– 19	1	0
20– 39	4	3
40– 59	20	28
60– 79	51	50
80–100	25	20
Total	101	101

a. For sources, see note 3. Each Senator's score for each Congress he served in during this span of years was counted. Scores for 1961–62 were not available, as explained in note 3.

b. Scores for Senators from the thirteen states classified as "Southern" have been omitted.

those cases where leaders exceed members, is only 6 percentage points.) For the Democrats, the critics' charge seems well founded. The voting pattern of Democratic committee leaders differs markedly from that of all Democratic Senators. The overall misrepresentation can be indexed as 18 percentage points, with fewer strong supporters and more weak supporters among committee leaders compared to the members at large.

What may be surprising, however, is that eliminating the Southerners does not change the Democratic pattern. Among *Northern* Democrats, there are still fewer strong supporters among the committee leaders and more weak supporters. The overall misrepresentation for Northern Democrats of 19 percentage points is almost identical to that for all Democrats.

Similar patterns are found for support of the President. Here the scores measure the per cent of times a congressman voted in support of identifiable presidential programs.[5] Republican committee leaders were more apt to mirror their party membership in supporting their President than Democratic committee leaders were. In the years 1953 through 1960, Republican Senate committee leaders supported Eisenhower's programs, on the average, 70 per cent of the time; all Republican Senators supported these programs 71 per cent of the time. For House Republican committee leaders, the average was 61 per cent; for all House Republicans, 64 per cent. In the years from 1961 through 1966, Senate Democratic chairmen supported Kennedy and Johnson programs on the average 51 per cent of the time; all Senate Democrats, 62 per cent; House Democratic chairmen, 64 per cent; and House Democratic members, 72 per cent.

These interparty differences hold also for the distribution of support of the President. Committee leaders in the Eisenhower Administration supported the President in similar proportions to the party membership as a whole. Democratic chairmen were weaker in support of Kennedy and Johnson programs than the Democratic members, and Northern Democratic chairmen were weaker than Northern Democratic congressional party members.[6]

If support of the Conservative Coalition* in Congress is taken as a measure of "conservatism" and "liberalism," one finds again an interparty difference. As the critics assert, the most conservative element in the Democratic party is awarded positions of committee leadership. However, the two Republican distributions are quite similar. It is true that the "most conservative element" is raised to leadership in that party also, but here it is the majority element. To illustrate, 49 per cent of Senate Republican committee leaders and 48 per cent of the membership opposed the Conservative Coalition from 0 to 10 per cent of the time. Of scant comfort to liberals, the fact remains that Republican committee leaders almost perfectly reflect the ideological distribution in their congressional party.

The Impact of Congressional Seniority

To what extent can the maverick voting behavior of Democratic chairmen, to the limited extent that it exists, be linked to the congressional seniority requirement— specifically, the greater length of service of these chairmen compared to others?

Table 20 presents the distribution of party support scores in the 88th Congress for all Senate Democrats (column 1); for "seniors" of ten or more years' consecutive service (column 2); for "seniors" who were also committee seniors in that they stayed on their committee of initial appointment (column 3); and for the chairmen (column 4). The results illustrate patterns found also for support of the President and of the Conservative Coalition.

The requirement of congressional seniority does make a difference, as a comparison of columns 1 and 2 shows. Seniors are less apt to support the party than are members as a whole. But

---

* The "Conservative Coalition" is traditionally defined as a grouping of congressmen in which a majority of Republicans and a majority of Southern Democrats oppose a majority of Northern Democrats. Voting with the coalition is therefore a conservative vote.

TABLE 20.   PARTY SUPPORT SCORES: MEMBERS, SENIORS,
COMMITTEE SENIORS, AND CHAIRMEN, SENATE DEMOCRATS,
1963-64[a]

Party Support Scores %	Members % (N=63)	Seniors % (N=25)	Seniors with No Committee Change % (N=15)	Chairmen % (N=16)
0–19	0	0	0	0
20–39	10	16	27	25
40–59	27	36	27	38
60–79	48	40	40	31
80–100	16	8	7	6
Total	101	100	101	100

a. All Senate Democrats are counted whose scores were available, excluding Senators from Alaska and Hawaii. While, theoretically, the numbers are too small to ensure that the particular percentage figures are meaningful, in this case the percentages have been included since they provide a clearer indication than the numbers alone of change in proportionate strength for each category.

committee seniors are even less loyal to the party than are congressional seniors. Note that in the lowest category of support (20 to 39 per cent), no senior congressmen changed committee. In other words, those loyal to the party were the most consistent in staying with their original committee assignment.

Yet the record of committee chairmen exhibits even less party loyalty than that of seniors. At each stage, then, of the process of selecting chairmen, the proportion of strong party supporters diminishes. Strong party supporters (those who fulfill the modest requirement that they support their party on at least 60 per cent of the roll calls) form 64 per cent of the congressional party membership, but supply only 37 per cent of the committee chairmen.

Differences in Northern Democratic Voting Behavior

THE TENDENCY TOWARD MAVERICK VOTING BEHAVior among *Northern* Democratic chairmen requires further attention. One possible explanation, which raises a larger question, is that differences in length of service—i.e., congressional seniority—may be related to differences in voting behavior, with the more senior Senators tending to weaker support for party and President than their junior colleagues. If relatively strong support for party and President is inversely related to length of congressional service, then the seniority system, which "disqualifies" the most junior members from a chance at the chairmanships, would be strengthening an antiparty, antipresidential, and "conservative" bias even outside the South.

This possibility can be investigated first by looking at the voting records of congressmen of different lengths of congressional service, excluding the South (see Table 21). One can

TABLE 21. SUPPORT OF THE PRESIDENT: SCORES OF NON-SOUTHERN DEMOCRATIC SENATORS BY LENGTH OF CONGRESSIONAL SERVICE[a]

Support Scores %	All Senators (N=133) %	Senators Elected Before			Chairmen (N=17) %
		1960 (N=108) %	1958 (N=71) %	1954 (N=59) %	
0– 19	0	0	0	0	0
20– 39	1	4	4	3	6
40– 59	23	25	30	31	47
60– 79	59	55	49	48	29
80–100	16	17	17	19	18
Total	99	101	100	101	100

a. The scores measure the per cent of times a Senator voted in support of Kennedy and Johnson programs in 1962, 1964, and 1965–66, as used in the analysis in an earlier section of the chapter. Numbers refer to the number of scores. Thus a congressman elected by 1960 would have three scores counted.

separate out from the full membership the scores of the most recent first-termers—Senators elected from 1960 on; then the scores of these first-termers plus the famous large class of 1958; then the scores of all Senators elected from 1954 on. This leaves a group of Senators of ten or more years' service, most nearly approximating the congressional tenure of committee leaders. Table 21 takes the distribution of scores on supporting the President for chairmen and members as presented in the earlier discussion and adds the distribution for these three intervening stages of seniority. Support of the President is selected since this aspect of voting behavior showed the greatest difference between Northern (i.e., non-Southern) Democratic committee leaders and members. If congressional seniority is related to voting behavior, one would expect considerable change in percentages between columns 1 and 2 or 1 and 3. Removing the scores of the most junior members would be expected to move the percentage much closer to that for committee leaders, whatever level of voting support is being considered.

Although some tendency in this direction is evident, the overall difference between committee leaders and members is not satisfactorily accounted for by differences in length of service. Committee leaders still differ considerably from the most senior Senators as regards their support for presidential programs. Some factor or factors other than congressional seniority is needed to explain this difference.[7]

In this case, the relatively weak support for the President among Northern (i.e., non-Southern) committee leaders may well be idiosyncratic—a combination of the small number of scores available for analysis and the large portion of those scores from congressmen from two states (Arizona and New Mexico). The "Southwest syndrome" observable here is curious. Dennis Chavez of New Mexico had a score of 31 per cent; Clinton Anderson, scores of 46, 49, and 59 per cent; and Carl Hayden, scores of 69, 46, and 40 per cent, accounting for much of the weak support.

The influence of congressional seniority can be examined further in the relationship between "liberal" voting by Northern Senators (opposition to the Conservative Coalition) and differences in congressional seniority, and between "liberal" voting and regional differences.

Tables 22 and 23, taken together, show some relationship between liberal voting and congressional seniority but perhaps stronger support for the relationship between liberal voting and regional differences. In the left-hand columns of Table 22, the

71

TABLE 22. "LIBERAL" VOTING OF NON-SOUTHERN DEMOCRATIC SENATORS, 1963–64, BY LENGTH OF SENATORIAL SERVICE

Senate Service (Years)	Northern Senators "Liberal"		Northern Senators Excluding the West "Liberal"	
	No.	Score[a]	No.	Score
20 or more	1	40	0	—
15– 19	2	61	0	—
10—14	7	69	4	77
5— 9	7	65	5	68
0— 4	22	74	17	75

a. Mean per cent opposed to the Conservative Coalition.

TABLE 23. "LIBERAL" VOTING OF NON-SOUTHERN DEMOCRATIC SENATORS, 1963–64, BY REGION AND LENGTH OF SERVICE

Region and Years Senate Service	No. of Senators	"Liberal" Scores	
		Mean % Opposed to Conservative Coalition	Median % Opposed to Conservative Coalition
East			
More than 4	3	77	78
4 or less	8	74	80
Total	11	75	78
Midwest			
More than 4	6	69	76
4 or less	9	76	81
Total	15	73	77
West			
More than 4	8	57	60
4 or less	5	71	79
Total	13	62	61

mean score of opposition to the Conservative Coalition increases as years of senatorial service decrease. But the degree of "liberalism," as measured here, can also be explained by regional differences. Western Democrats exhibit *both* less "liberal" voting[8] and more congressional tenure. Interpretation is complicated by the fact that length of service follows regional lines. The East and Midwest are newer in their allegiance to the Democratic party.[9] As Table 22 shows, the relationship between length of service and liberal voting disappears with the removal of the Western Senators.

Table 23 provides some evidence linking voting behavior to length of service when regional differences are controlled for. In the West and Midwest, junior Senators are more liberal in voting; in the East, they are about the same.

Republican Senators in 1963–64, by the way, exhibited *no* relationship betwen length of service and liberal voting[10] but showed a regional difference. The East in the Republican party stands alone in its opposition to the Conservative Coalition. Mean scores by region were: East, 44 per cent; Midwest, 8 per cent; South, 15 per cent; and West, 9 per cent.[11]

The weight of evidence suggests that, while length of service among Northern Democrats may be a secondary factor in explaining voting behavior, regional differences are a stronger factor. Length of service could not account for the curious difference between Northern Democratic chairmen and members in support of the President or the smaller difference between them in support of the party. While some evidence links the more junior Senators with more liberal voting, regional differences seem even more important in explaining degrees of liberalism and conservatism. Based on the slight evidence available, a criticism of the seniority system could claim that it benefits those Northern Democrats, mainly in the West, who tend to be less "liberal" in their voting behavior than their more junior Northern colleagues. But it would have to be a cautiously stated argument.

It seems that a number of separate factors combine to explain the fact that the voting records of Democratic committee leaders are often out of line with the position of their party. The predominance of Southerners in the senior membership of the party is one factor; on this point the critics are correct. But committee changes and the luck or discretion involved in original assignments have worked in the same direction. And even among Northern Democrats, the relative advantage given Western Senators, weakest in party loyalty among the Northerners, has reinforced the general tendency. By this view, congressional seniority is only one of several factors which produce a conservative cast in the Democratic chairmen.

The Chairmen: After Landslide Presidential Elections

THE GENERAL CLAIM OF AN ANTIPARTY, ANTIPRESIdential bias built into the seniority system subsumes another which, in many observers' view, may be the more serious indictment. Operating with such a bias, the seniority system creates a leadership corps guaranteed to frustrate electoral mandates when a new President is elected and his party takes over control of Congress. The new Administration must face the old guard of the party, firmly entrenched in committee chairs. George Galloway's description is a standard one:

A majority of the membership of the House may come fresh from the people with a clear mandate for a program of social action, only to see their attempts to keep their promises frustrated and their bills whittled away or pigeonholed by a little group of committee chairmen who were first elected to Congress a generation ago on issues now settled and forgotten and who have risen to dominate the key committees.[12]

The issue of representativeness is posed implicitly: a "majority of the membership" is contrasted with "a little group of committee chairmen." That majority is "fresh from the people" in contrast to the little group who "were first elected . . . a generation ago."

Even if the claim is valid, the threat may well be overstated, since only twice in the past forty years could such a situation have occurred. In 1932 and 1952 the American electorate not only overwhelmingly elected Presidents, judging by both popular and electoral vote; they also gave them Congresses controlled by their parties. It may be worth while to examine presidential-congressional relations following these two elections, even though the first of the two is outside the twenty-year span used for most of this study. To what extent did the committee chairmen exhibit policy stands in Congress which tended to oppose the new congressional majority or the new President?

The charge as stated is difficult to investigate. One can recite a series of examples of "obstructionism" and "pigeonholing," retell the story of Chairman Smith's burned barn which allegedly kept him from holding civil rights hearings, but one has not proven any general case by such examples. Indeed, the most successful kinds of obstructionism could not be documented at all—cases where a powerful chairman's known opposition to a program caused it to be dropped or seriously modified before it ever left the White House. Clearly any detailed program-by-program analysis of the Administrations of Roosevelt and Eisenhower is beyond the scope of this study. Perhaps the best way to approach the subject is to try to gain some clear impression of what was meant by "support" of or "opposition" to the President in certain Administrations. It is possible to describe a climate of receptivity or opposition to presidential programs which permeates Capitol Hill, and to appraise the committee chairmen's attitudes in relation to this climate of opinion. This should provide an indication at least of whether conditions for obstructionism were present. Finally, by seeing what observers consider to be the ultimate success or failure of the presidential programs, one can gain some idea of how effective this opposition was.

The year 1933 saw a new Democratic party government formed—with F.D.R. in the White House and Southerners in almost all of the major committee chairs in Congress. Considering the same "major" standing committees for 1921–46 which were used in earlier portions of the study, there were ten Southerners in the eleven major committee posts in the House. (John Mead of New York chaired the Post Office Committee.) There were seven Southerners in the eleven major committee posts in the Senate. The incongruity is striking and could easily lead one to conclude with Galloway that the contrast in *constituency* implied an opposition in *policy*. But according to most accounts of the first Roosevelt Administration, no such opposition existed.

First of all, there was no clear-cut opposition in policy orientation. In the early 1930's, the South was neither against Roosevelt nor against the New Deal proposals.[13] Indeed, F.D.R. considered himself an "adopted" Southerner with a second home in Georgia. Without Southern support, he would not have been nominated in 1932. Nine states of the South supported him. Southern delegates looked to Roosevelt as a candidate who could deliver them from Smith and the Eastern conservative domination of the Democratic party. Both defeated rivals— Smith and Garner—were considered more conservative than Roosevelt. It must be remembered that the South in 1933 was not noticeably "conservative" in domestic policy. The Southern economy badly needed a nationally sponsored program of economic recovery and reform. Indeed, such Southern leaders as Tom Connally and Huey Long were worried that Roosevelt would be too conservative. One further point might be added. Southerners were not restricted to the committee chairs of Congress. There were even three Southerners in the cabinet—Hull, Roper, and Swanson.

Second, there was really no serious Democratic opposition in major policy in the first Roosevelt Administration. Carter Glass might grumble as he did it, but he helped steer the necessary economic legislation through the Congress. In fact, the Southern leadership in Congress helped the Roosevelt Administration enact its enormous amount of reform legislation. The time was too busy—too "emergency-conscious"—for intraparty squabbles. By the time Congress caught its breath and remembered its historic duty to criticize Presidents, the criticism seems to have come mainly from Western progressives.[14] Clearly, the first Roosevelt Administration gives no support for the stereotype of committee "barons"—outnumbered, outmoded, and yet still powerful—who are sworn to frustrate presidential proposals.

It was the *second* Roosevelt Administration that brought severe strains to presidential-legislative relations, and the birth of the modern "conservative" opposition. But even here, the chairmen cannot be distinguished from the general "congressional conservatism" which emerged. Rexford Tugwell describes a "conservative veto"—essentially a Southern veto—in the 1937–38 session, against which F.D.R. was helpless. He lost the antilynching bill, saw the crippling of the Farm Security Administration and the defeat of his tax proposals.[15] Roosevelt's fight over the Supreme Court bill consolidated Southern and conservative opposition and, by the midterm elections of 1938, the break between Roosevelt and Southern conservatives was complete. Roosevelt's attempted purge of Southern conservatives is associated in most accounts with his strong feelings over opposition to his Court fight,[16] but it also served the purpose of delineating the President's view of the line between Democratic liberals and conservatives. According to Frank Freidel, by the late 1930's only a "slim majority" of Southern congressmen remained loyal to the President.[17]

What of the committee chairmen in all this, as Roosevelt and the Democratic South began to go their separate ways? It seems that some of the committee chairmen formed a part—but only a part—of the conservative opposition. The three candidates Roosevelt attempted to purge in the Democratic primaries of 1938 were all Southerners—Senators George, Smith, and Tydings. Only one—Ellison Smith of South Carolina—was a committee chairman.[18] Rexford Tugwell quotes Roosevelt's reference to a "hater's club" in Congress, consisting of such men as Wheeler, McCarran, Tydings, Glass, and John J. O'Connor.[19] But only one of these—Carter Glass of Virginia—was a committee chairman. It seems fair to conclude that, in the midst of growing congressional opposition and criticism of the second Roosevelt Administration, some of the committee leaders of Congress also opposed and criticized Roosevelt proposals. In this, they seem to have been more or less representative of the Democratic party and the congressional branch of government of the time.

The second example of an electoral mandate bringing a change in party control—the first Eisenhower Administration—was rather different. From the beginning, the President faced a Congress far from congenial. Eisenhower, himself, describes the "stern facts" facing him on the legislative side. The Republicans had a very slim majority in both houses. In the House, they had an eleven-seat margin. In the Senate, the situation was even tighter. The Republican party had won 48 seats; the Democrats, 47; and there was Independent Wayne Morse, who usually voted with the Democrats. In addition, as Eisenhower remarks, he faced a congressional majority party completely inexperienced in working with an executive. No Republican Senator in the 1953–54 Congress had ever served with a President of his party. And of all the Republicans in the House, only fifteen could remember serving with a Republican President.[20] Speaker of the House Joseph Martin admits that he and the rest of the Republicans "had a difficult time shedding the psychology of opposition."[21]

Eisenhower touches only tangentially the "wide variety of political views" represented in the congressional Republican party, though this was one of the "sternest facts" of all. The fact is, of course, that two main views were represented, commonly referred to as "modern Republicanism," which had selected Eisenhower as its champion, and the older-style Republicanism preached and practiced by Robert Taft. According to Speaker Martin, this latter group found modern Republicanism "too similar to the Roosevelt and Truman policies [the Republicans] had been accustomed to opposing."[22] These two factions had fought it out at the Republican convention in 1952. It is not an exaggeration to say that in 1953 the winning candidate and his view of Republicanism controlled the White House, while the losing Republican candidate and his view controlled the Congress. As Richard Rovere points out, not only the Senate but also the House leadership was dominated by Taft supporters.

Certainly the Republicans taking over the committee chairs

in Congress were not striking examples of "modern Republicanism." House chairmen Taber, Reed, Allen, and Velde were staunchly conservative. Senators Millikin (Finance), Butler (Interior), Bridges (Appropriations), and Knowland (succeeding Taft on Foreign Relations) were all Taft followers. According to Eisenhower's autobiography, Senators Butler (Interior), Jenner (Rules), and McCarthy (Government Operations) were from the beginning outspoken critics of his policies; and Millikin and Bridges could not normally be relied on to support Eisenhower programs.[23]

With such a composition of the Congress, it is not surprising that the Eisenhower Administration faced opposition from the start. In Robert Donovan's words, "the honeymoon with Congress which traditionally is supposed to ease a new President through his early days never seemed to materialize for Eisenhower, who tried more than many Presidents have done to cooperate with the legislative branch."[24] The Administration immediately faced opposition on the Bohlen appointment as ambassador to Russia. (Bohlen had sat next to F.D.R. at Yalta.) Of the 13 Senators finally voting against the appointment, 11 were Republicans. Three of these were chairmen—Bricker, Bridges, and McCarthy. The Administration also faced a fight on the proposed Bricker Amendment, named for the Chairman of the Commerce Committee. Even though Eisenhower had sent a letter to the Senate stating he was "unalterably opposed" to the amendment, it missed only by a close vote. The only slightly tempered substitute amendment missed by only one vote and even got the support of Knowland himself. And one of the biggest headaches of the Eisenhower Administration involved Senator McCarthy, himself a committee chairman.

In what is a classic illustration of the obstructionist power of committee chairmen, House Ways and Means Chairman Reed waged one of the strongest fights against the new Administration on its tax proposals. Reed, who favored cutting taxes immediately, kept Eisenhower's proposed extension of the excess-profits tax in his committee and resisted Administration persuasion to bring it to a committee vote. After lengthy efforts by House leaders Martin and Halleck and others, the Rules Committee finally voted to bring the Administration bill to the floor without the approval of Ways and Means. Only at this point did Reed capitulate and let the bill go out of committee on its way to become law.[25]

In the long run, the 1953–54 Congress did pass most of the Eisenhower program. Of 19 major programs, Congress gave the President all or most of what he asked for on 13, including legislation increasing social security benefits and unemployment insurance, government programs for foreign aid, highways, vocational rehabilitation, and housing. And these programs, it is clear, were not the kind to cause rejoicing in traditional Republican circles. Eisenhower did not get health reinsurance or a reduction in tariffs, among others.[26] By the way, Eisenhower's failure on tariffs can be attributed in large part to the resistance of Senate Finance Chairman Eugene Millikin, well known for strong protectionist views. In this resistance, of course, he had far-ranging Republican support. Perhaps a fair summary of the 1953–54 relations between President and Congress is that, while the Administration did manage to secure congressional support for a majority of its proposals, it had to fight hard to get it. "Fighting" here included gaining the support of a number of congressional Democrats.

The 1953–54 experience seems to provide stronger support for the conventional charge than the New Deal experience usually cited. A new Administration was confronted with an old party leadership, remembering old ways and distrustful of the "new," which, after all, was a word used in capitals by the Democrats. Yet it should be stressed that the committee chairmen were by no means alone—a "little group" opposed to the "fresh majority" in the Congress. Their skepticism and opposition were shared by the elected leadership in Congress—by such men as Taft, Knowland, and Halleck—and by a sizable portion of the whole congressional Republican party. The clear-cut opposition here between "presidential liberalism" (in this case, "moderatism") and "congressional conservatism" found the committee chairmen with the party leadership in Congress right where they might be expected—on the congressional side.

These impressions, taken together, may illustrate merely the well-known ambivalence between President and Congress and the diversity and hospitality of the American political parties, rather than any special effects of the seniority system. In times of emergency, no seniority system (or any other congressional practice, for that matter) is going to keep Congress from supplying the President with the support he needs. Once the emergency is over, relations between the two branches return to normal, "normal" meaning the usual mixture of co-operation and conflict between the presidency and the "proud, jealous, watchful co-ordinate branch" which is the Congress.[27] After landslide elections, the time lag that the seniority system builds into the congressional committee leadership does not seem to cause the committee chairmen to act any differently toward a new President than the congressional party as a whole. It may well be that the clearest examples of opposition occur following close elections, where the country and even the majority party are divided, where a number of congressmen feel they "owe" the President nothing because they won despite his presence at the top of the ticket. Perhaps 1961–62 would reveal more clear opposition by committee chairmen than the three "mandated" Administrations that have been considered. But even there, that opposition may be merely representative of wider congressional feeling. In any case, the fear that the seniority system frustrates clear electoral mandates does not seem supported by the foregoing examples. At least, no *special* perversity of the committee chairmen seems evident.

Summary

COMMITTEE LEADERS DO INDEED APPEAR TO BE "conservative" and slightly less likely in the Democratic party, but not in the Republican party, to support party and presidential programs. Only in the Democratic party could the recorded policy stands of chairmen be said to "misrepresent" the membership (and even there the two distributions of scores—for chairmen and for all Democrats—were roughly congruent). Indeed, Republican committee leaders produced a strikingly close reflection of their party's membership in support for party programs and in liberal-conservative voting. The fact that chairmen tended to be unrepresentative in one party and representative in the other permits no inference that the seniority system *per se* produces either effect. The point may be qualified as follows. In the Democratic party, the requirement of congressional seniority gave to the South and the West, regions of greatest Democratic strength to start with, an increased advantage, and these areas tended to be weakest in "liberalism" and support for presidential Democratic programs. But congressional seniority is only one factor contributing to the conservative cast of Democratic chairmen. Most notably conservative Democrats, weakest in support of party programs, were more likely to stay with their committees than their more liberal colleagues—suggesting that patterns of initial assignment or subsequent changes also influenced the results.

And yet a detailed examination of two Congresses does not support the claim that chairmen will obstruct proposals of a new President, elected by a landslide, to any noticeable extent beyond the average congressional membership. That more extreme statement cannot be made. If one can characterize congressional party attitudes toward Presidents—strongly supportive in 1931–32; considerably more critical in 1937–38; downright suspicious in 1953–54—then the stances taken by chairmen seem well in line with the more widespread congressional response.

VI

The Chairmen and Their Committees

ONE FINAL QUESTION NEEDS ATTENTION. How well do chairmen represent the committees they head? The subject deserves full-length treatment in itself, but at least a preliminary outline can be offered here. It will consider the following points: (1) Can variations in policy leanings on a committee-by-committee basis be identified? (2) If so, is there evidence suggesting that committee members, including the chairman, tend to be assigned to that committee on the basis of these policy leanings? In other words, does the process of committee assignment tend to build in a similarity among committee members in constituency interests or other shared goals which would give the majority a similar outlook regarding the committee's business? If so, the chairman may automatically tend to be representative of the committee as a whole. (3) Where no such similarity exists, what are the powers of, and constraints on, chairmen that might allow them to act in opposition to a committee majority or might inhibit them from so acting? Answers to these questions should provide some sense of the range of representativeness or the reverse possible for chairmen in the substantive concerns of their own committees.

Committees, it should be noted, are bipartisan creatures. The committee "majority" necessary for a quorum or a vote may be drawn from members of both parties. And so presumably a chairman could act in accord with a committee majority and yet in opposition to his party's majority on the committee.

Consider the case of a Southern Democratic chairman of a committee composed of ten Democrats and seven Republicans. Seven Northern liberal Democrats could find themselves a minority on some issues if their three Democratic colleagues sided with at least six of the Republicans. Two different majorities are thus possible: the bipartisan voting majority and the party majority. Since critics of the seniority system are particularly concerned with how well a chairman represents his party, both majorities will be considered, where relevant, in the discussion that follows.

The Committee System and Committee Assignments

THE DIVISION OF CONGRESSIONAL LABOR INTO twenty House and sixteen Senate standing committees with specific subject matter jurisdictions tends to produce a committee system that mirrors national policy concerns. Considerable overlapping of jurisdiction exists. A number of committees may share a policy area, such as economic legislation; and one committee may consider a number of disparate policy concerns. The Senate Banking and Currency Committee, for example, considers not only banking and currency but also public and private housing, mass transportation, and area redevelopment. Nevertheless, the fact that committees have identifiable policy areas means that congressmen may seek committee assignments congenial to their own interests in national policy. Since a number of congressmen would share the same interests—whether the building of dams, the growing of crops, or the fighting of Communists at home or abroad—these congressmen might well find themselves with like-minded colleagues on a committee.

Of course, to seek a committee assignment is not necessarily to get it. Assignment of new members to committees and of members seeking transfers is made by the Committee on Committees in each of the four congressional parties. For House Democrats, the Ways and Means Committee Democrats perform the task of committee assignment. The other three congressional parties select committees for that specific purpose. In general, the Committee on Committees will try to satisfy a congressman's preference. One important criterion is said to be the congressman-constituency relationship. Assignments accord with what will help a congressman back home, particularly as regards reelection.[1] Thus, where possible, a congressman whose constituency is concerned with keeping a major naval base, raising hogs, or initiating a new large-scale reclamation project may find his way fairly easily to Armed Services, Agriculture, or Interior, respectively. It is a rare case when a Shirley Chisholm finds herself assigned to Agriculture and Forestry— not exactly a burning concern of her New York City district.

Other influences also affect committee assignments. One important criterion is geography. On the key House committees of Appropriations, Rules, and Ways and Means, this means that some attempt is made to secure assignments for congressmen from each of the major regions of the nation. On other committees, geographical representation means that upon retirement of a congressman from a certain state, another congressman from that state is appointed to the committee. Thus Texas has been represented on the Ways and Means Committee for more than two decades. Ohio remains on the House Public Works Committee.

Party leaders also may exert considerable influence on the selections. Speaker Sam Rayburn, for years, kept a watchful eye on Ways and Means Committee assignments to ensure that members would be favorable to reciprocal trade agreements and opposed to changes in the oil depletion allowance. House party leaders have guarded assignment to the three key House committees to ensure that moderate, "responsible" legislators, able to compromise and devoted to the congressional institution, would be chosen.[2] A member should also be from a district sufficiently safe to permit him the luxury of compromising. For all committees in the House, senior members of a state delegation may influence the assignment of a freshman from the state.[3] And according to one student of congressional committees, it is common practice to clear potential appointees with the committee chairman.[4]

All this suggests that at least on some committees the process of assignment may ensure that a substantial portion of the membership is marked by similarity in constituencies, attitudes toward the legislative process, and general policy goals. That would seem most likely on some "interest" committees and the House "prestige" committees, although considerable work on the subject on a committee-by-committee basis remains to be done. The criterion of constituency representation, the selection of certain types of legislator for key committees, and clearance with the chairman, as well as the self-selection involved in the member's own stated preference—all tend to induce some such similarity. It may then follow that chairmen, subjected to the same process of selection and in part influencing later selections, might share policy goals concerning their committees' subject matter with a substantial portion of the members.

The point should not be overstressed. Some committees, consciously or unconsciously, seem prone to *dissimilarity*. Here the process of committee assignment builds in conflict. Thus Banking and Currency may attract both big bank and anti-big-bank, pro-Federal Reserve and anti-Federal Reserve interests. The most notable instance of this kind is the House Education and Labor Committee, which has tended to recruit pro-labor Democrats and pro-management Republicans. Southerners on the committee have been concerned with integrated schooling. And by tradition, a Roman Catholic is appointed to the committee out of concern for the question of aid to private schools. But according to Nicholas Masters in his study of House committee assignments, the Education and Labor Committee is a special case—producing a "standoff between antagonists." Masters reports that "as the party committees have seen it in recent years, this assignment is no place for a neutral when there are so many belligerents around."[5]

Some additional insight can be gained by looking at variation in committees on general policy and comparing this with

TABLE 24.   CORRESPONDENCE BETWEEN CHAIRMEN AND
PARTY MAJORITIES: HOUSE AND SENATE COMMITTEES
OF THE 87TH CONGRESS

Chair-man	Party Majority	House Committees	Senate Committees
Southern	Southern	Agriculture	Agriculture
		Armed Services	Armed Services
		District of Columbia	Finance
		Post Office	Judiciary
		Rules	Post Office
		Veterans	
		No. of Cases = 6	**No. of Cases = 5**
Northern	Northern	Appropriations	Commerce
		Education and Labor	District of Columbia
		Foreign Affairs	Interior
		Government Operations	Public Works
		Interior	Rules
		Judiciary	
		Public Works	
		Un-American Activities	
		No. of Cases = 8	**No. of Cases = 5**
Southern	Northern	Banking and Currency	Banking and Currency
		House Administration	Foreign Relations
		Commerce	Government Operations
		Merchant Marine	Labor
		Science	Space
		Ways and Means	
		No. of Cases = 6	**No. of Cases = 5**
Northern	Southern		Appropriations
		No. of Cases = 0	**No. of Cases = 1**

the variation in chairmen. As Froman[6] shows, in the 88th Congress conservative chairmen tended to head conservative committees. In this Congress there were only three Senate committees where a combination of Southern Democrats and Republicans did not equal a majority or only one less than a majority. These were Commerce, Interior, and Public Works. In the House, there was only one such committee—Education and Labor. The chairman in each of these exceptional cases was a northern liberal Democrat: Magnuson (Washington) of

Commerce; Jackson (Washington) of Interior; McNamara (Michigan) of Public Works; and Powell (New York) of House Education and Labor.

Considering only the Democratic committee members, a comparable tendency can be observed. Committees with a majority of Northern Democrats tend to have Northern chairmen, while committees with a Southern majority have Southern chairmen. A number of exceptions do exist. But as Table 24 shows, the cases of correspondence beween chairmen and their party majorities far outnumber the cases of difference. This pattern holds for both Senate and House committees.[7]

It was mentioned in Chapter III that by the early 1960's the relative decrease in Southern members of the Democratic congressional parties was not yet reflected in the chairmanships. Despite this time lag built in by the seniority system, Table 24 makes clear that on a committee-by-committee basis, a majority of chairmen were regionally representative of their committees. And of the six House committees having a Southern chairman with a Northern party majority, three had a Northerner as the second-ranking majority party member. Of the five Senate committees in that category, two had a Northerner next in line.

Other points of interest deserve mention. Note that the top three "prestigious" House committees fall in three separate categories. There is also an intriguing similarity between House and Senate patterns of correspondence. In both chambers, Agriculture, Armed Services, and Post Office committees fall in the Southern-Southern category. Public Works and Interior fall in the Northern-Northern category. And Banking and Currency and the Science committees fall in the Southern-Northern category.

The Role of the Chairman

THE PRECEDING SECTION SUGGESTS THAT IN A NUMber of committees the chairmen will be like a substantial portion of the members. But where no such likeness exists, what powers of the chairmen might permit them to act against the views of the committee? What constraints might prevent them from doing so? Chairmen have a number of impressive procedural powers which allow them to exert their individual influences on legislation being considered in committee. They set the times and frequencies for committee meetings, determine the agenda, schedule hearings, and preside. They determine the number and the jurisdiction of subcommittees and appoint subcommittee chairmen and members. They influence the selection of conference committee members. They decide the size and business of the committee staff. Of course, a chairman cannot report a bill favorably if a majority of the committee votes against it. But he has considerable means at his disposal, particularly in agenda-setting and choice of subcommittee chairmen, to persuade necessary members to his way of thinking. And through his control over scheduling, he has the power to stop a bill from coming to what would otherwise be a favorable vote.

Despite this potential power to act in an arbitrary, individual fashion, observers agree that "one-man rule" on a committee is not the normal situation.[8] Congressmen expect cooperation and consultation between chairmen and members. The threat of disruption and the possibility, however unlikely, of a committee revolt against a chairman further tend to restrict any clearly arbitrary rule. As Charles Jones says of both committee and party leaders, "the leader who maintains himself in a responsible position of authority over a long period of time must be adaptive, communicative, accommodating, and accountable."[9] The point deserves some elaboration.

Numerous instances can be cited where chairmen have used their procedural powers in an independent fashion to influence legislative results. The famous story is told of Rules Chairman Howard Smith's delay in scheduling hearings for a rule on civil rights legislation in the 88th Congress. Smith was home in Virginia inspecting a "burned barn." The retort attributed to

Sam Rayburn is that he knew Judge Smith might do a lot of things to stop civil rights legislation, but he did not think he would resort to arson. A. Willis Robertson, Chairman of the Senate Banking and Currency Committee, used the full panoply of his powers in protecting certain big-banking interests and the Federal Reserve. For instance, Robertson abolished the subcommittee on the Federal Reserve System when it became known that Senators Clark and Proxmire were planning to use that base for a critical review of Federal Reserve policy.[10] Robertson's delay in scheduling hearings on the Truth-in-Lending Bill in the 88th Congress, the special concern of committee member Paul Douglas, provoked Douglas to bring the matter to the full Senate's attention on the floor.

Perhaps the most vivid illustration of a chairman's use of obstructionist power concerns Graham Barden, Chairman of the House Education and Labor Committee and arch-foe of federal aid to education. In the words of one Democratic committee member, "Barden was trying to keep things from being done," and committee liberals and conservatives agreed he was eminently successful. Among other tactics, Barden refused to schedule regular meetings. A committee member recalled a first meeting one year in April and the next one in June. He would terminate meetings by declaring the absence of a quorum. One colleague recalls an occasion when the committee had recessed for a roll call vote on the floor. Barden stayed behind, giving instructions to his assistant to call back when the roll call was over. The colleague continues:

I was one of the first ones back, and Barden was sitting there. He got a phone call, put down the phone, looked around and said, "No quorum" and banged the gavel. I jumped up and protested. He said, "No quorum," and left. . . . Technically he was right. We were supposed to be sitting during debate and should have begun when the floor debate began again. . . . The timetable was such that if we didn't complete our work that day we couldn't meet for some time.[11]

At another time on an education bill, he called in 92 witnesses from the Chamber of Commerce and was going to let them all talk. Remarked one liberal committee member, "We learned a lot from Barden."[12]

Yet in each of these cases the Democrats on the committees were themselves deeply divided: on the Rules Committee, between Northern liberals and Southern conservatives; in Banking and Currency, between banking and small business interests as well as between liberals and conservatives.[13] The conflict-ridden Education and Labor Committee was fractionalized on education bills by issues of federal aid, parochial schools, and segregation.[14] These were not cases in which a chairman acted against the wishes of a clear majority of the committee or of his own party. Moreover, even these cases of independent action by chairmen were sufficiently far from usual congressional practice to bring repercussions. Committee members do not often take to the Senate floor to complain about their chairmen. Committee revolts are rare, but liberal Democrats, increased in number by the 1958 elections, managed to wrest power from Barden in the 85th Congress. Judge Smith's handling of bills in the Rules Committee during the late 1950's was used as an argument in the fight to expand the Rules Committee in 1961.

In contrast, cases can also be cited of close cooperation between chairmen and committee members. Richard Fenno has documented the patterns of consultation on the House Appropriations Committee, particularly between the chairman and subcommittee chairmen and the chairmen and ranking minority members.[15] The ability of Carl Vinson, Armed Services Committee Chairman, to gain unanimous committee reports on controversial legislation has already been noted. One of the best illustrations is provided by Wilbur Mills, Chairman of the key House Committee on Ways and Means. Both Democrats and Republicans on the committee agree that Mills runs Ways and Means by seeking a consensus. He will "compromise, bargain, cajole, swap, bend, plead, amend, coax, and unite until as much of the controversy as possible is drained from the bill, and as many members of the Committee as possible support it."[16]

There is a particularly close working relationship between Mills and ranking minority member Byrnes. Yet members agree that the committee has a head. In this case, Mills' influence with the committee appears to be closely connected with his perception and the members' perception that he is accountable to them. John F. Manley summarizes his study of Mills as follows: "The decisions of the Committee are shaped and articulated by Mills, but if his word comes close to being law in the Committee it is because he has listened well to the words of others."[17]

A more thorough committee-by-committee study would be necessary to make the point conclusively, but on balance the degree of a chairman's responsiveness to his committee apparently varies with the cohesiveness of the majority party and of the full committee and with the individual style of the chairman. It is perhaps this variety which prompted the Joint Committee on the Organization of Congress (1965–66) to urge standardization of committee procedures on the following lines: (1) fixing of regular meetings; (2) allowing the most senior majority party member to preside over committee meetings should the chairman be absent; (3) prohibiting voting to report a bill unless a committee majority is present; and (4) requiring that the chairman file a committee report no later than seven days after the committee has voted on the bill.[18] Each of these points touches on the chairman's procedural power to influence legislation. While congressional expectations appear to inhibit a chairman's use of arbitrary power, they have evidently been flexible enough to permit some variation in practice.

Summary

TAKEN TOGETHER, THIS SURVEY SUGGESTS THAT while chairmen have the power to "misrepresent" the wishes of the committee membership, a number of factors tend to preclude or inhibit such action for some if not all committees. The process of committee assignment tends to bring together congressmen, including the chairman, who are like-minded on committee policy. Party leaders may strengthen this tendency on some key committees by intervening so that only certain kinds of congressmen are appointed. While by contrast some committees seem deliberately to build in dissimilarity and conflict, a first sounding of the subject suggests that this is not the normal pattern. The practice of clearing new committee assignments with the chairman concerned, to the extent that it is followed, strengthens the likelihood that committee members, including the chairman, can find common ground or shared goals.

Finally, there appear to be congressional expectations governing the behavior of chairmen which would further inhibit any clear-cut misrepresentation of a committee's views on policy even in cases where there is no basic similarity between chairmen and members. Some of the most influential chairmen are also the most attentive to their committee members. Instances of excessively independent action by chairmen, even with no clear opposing majority in the committee or the party, have brought repercussions. While committees appear to vary considerably in the degree of responsiveness expected of the chairman, that variation itself indicates that the chairman-committee relationship resists stereotyping.

VII

Committee Leaders and Party Leaaers

ANOTHER KIND OF LEADERSHIP SELECTION takes place in Congress—selection of party leaders in House and Senate. It may usefully be compared with the seniority system both for the method of selection and for the leaders it selects. The methods of selection are quite different; to what extent and in what ways is there nevertheless a similarity between the leaders selected? Such a comparison should help place the seniority system in clearer perspective, and incidentally extend our knowledge of the structure of congressional leadership.

Reformist commentaries imply a distinction between the two kinds of leader when they propose to select chairmen by nomination of the party leader—the Speaker of the House or the Majority Leader of the Senate. According to Representative Bolling, the leader's "ability to veto or to replace a man completely out of step with his party viewpoint . . . would give pause to the Member who would bolt his party's program."[1] Such proposals assume that party leaders would disregard seniority and nominate candidates for chairmen who were more congenial than the present chairmen to the majority of the congressional party. Yet seniority norms govern both selection processes, and produce two groups who have grown up together in Congress. The party leaders may be as sensitive to the claims of seniority as their colleagues in the committee chairs. The point can be tentatively explored by tracing similarities in career patterns, constituency characteristics, and policy positions. The two groups, while different in many ways, exhibit significant similarities.

Career Patterns

ONE POINT OF DIFFERENCE IS READILY APPARENT. The selection of party leaders is, ostensibly at least, less automatic than the selection of chairmen. When a vacancy occurs for Speaker or for the floor leaders in the House, new leaders are elected by the party caucus. (The Speaker is then chosen officially by a vote of the entire House.) Majority and Minority Leaders in the Senate are also elected by their party in caucus, there called the Party Conference. Such a wider latitude is also observable at an earlier point in the recruitment of party leaders. The selection of Whip in both Senate and House parties, a position which may serve as a stepping-stone to a higher party position, permits the congressional party to exercise more control over the selection process than does the automatic system of selecting committee chairmen.

The two selection systems, however, are similar in two ways. Both are rooted in the *party* organization in Congress and are thus dependent, although in different ways, on congressional party membership. Committee seniority is arranged by party lists; its distribution is greatly influenced by the distribution of membership, as pointed out throughout this study. Party leadership is determined by vote of the party in caucus—with results, again, influenced by congressional party membership, a point that will be made clearer below.

Second, even in the selection of party leaders congressional seniority is important. According to Robert L. Peabody's study of party leadership in the House, a representative must have "substantial service, a minimum of five terms, before he can be considered a candidate for leadership." Speaking of qualifications for party leadership in the House, Representative Clem

Miller remarked: "Above all, in the House, one must *last*."[2]
The extent to which seniority shapes party leadership as well
as committee leadership is explored below. Party leaders are
taken to include House Speakers, Majority and Minority Leaders, and the two chief party Whips; Senate Majority and Minority Leaders and the two Whips. All leaders serving during
the 1947–1966 period are included.

TABLE 25.   PARTY LEADERS AND COMMITTEE LEADERS DURING 1947–66
COMPARED ON SOME POINTS OF "SENIORITY"

	Median Age of Leadership (during terms of service)		Median No. Years to Gain Leadership		Median No. Years in Leadership Position	
	Party Leaders	CC's/ RMM's	Party Leaders	CC's/ RMM's	Party Leaders	CC's/ RMM's
DEMOCRATS						
Senate	60	66.0	10	10	6	8
House	62	65.5	21	16	16	6
REPUBLICANS						
Senate	64	63.5	11.5	7	3	4
House	62	62.5	16	12	8	6

Both groups are clearly congressional "seniors," as Table 25
shows. It is true that Democratic party leaders are on the
average somewhat younger than Democratic committee chairmen, although for the Republicans they average about the
same age. In three of the four congressional parties, party
leaders have had to spend even more years in Congress before
gaining leadership posts. And in the House, they stay longer
once there. In the House especially one can see that the path to
party leadership is a long one, which is begun early and pursued through the winning of many elections.

Given this similarity in congressional seniority, one might
expect that party leaders could have succeeded to committee
chairs also. In other words, the two different modes of selection
may be drawing from the same group of senior members of

Congress. This is to some extent true. Of the 11 party leaders who had received committee assignments during the 1947–1966 period, by the time of their elevation as party leader 4 were chairmen or ranking minority members, one held a second rank, and 3 a third rank on committees.[3] The one clear difference identified in career patterns between the two groups— the party leaders' tendency to change committees, with subsequent loss of the committee seniority[4]—can explain why even more party leaders had not attained top committee rank.

Second, career patterns for both groups are similar in that they include a recognized series of stages—apprenticeship posts—on the way to leadership. This situation of course is built in by the seniority system for committee chairmen. But it is also true for party leaders, although in that case the series of apprenticeship posts is greatly abbreviated to a two-step (Whip—Floor Leader) or three-step (Whip—Floor Leader— Speaker) process. The clearest instance of this is seen among House Democrats. Over the past two decades Rayburn held sway as Speaker: he was replaced after his death by Majority Leader McCormack, whose position as Floor Leader was filled in turn by Albert, the Majority Whip. But both Senate Democrats and Republicans have followed this recruitment pattern in at least one instance.[5]

The stability of the process is illustrated in Table 26, which lists occupants of these top party positions for the past two decades and indicates the instances when a departure from the normal apprenticeship process occurred: either (1) when a congressman was removed from his post; or (2) when he retained his post but was not raised to a vacant higher position.[6] An initial indicates that the same man continued in office or upon a vacancy was promoted from the next lower office. A change in incumbents for an office where no "departure from precedent" (small capitals) occurred indicates that the previous incumbent has left Congress—through death, retirement, or a move to the vice-presidency.

If one takes each of the nine Congresses from the 81st (1949–

TABLE 26. PARTY LEADERSHIP STABILITY, 1947–66

	80th Cong.	81st	82nd	83rd	84th	85th	86th	87th	88th	89th
HD 1	Rayburn	R	R	R	R	R	R	R	M	M
2	McCormack	M	M	M	M	M	M	M	A	A
3		Priest	P		Albert	A	A	A	Boggs	B
No. of departures: 0										
HR 1	Martin	M	M	M	M	M	HALLECK	H	H	FORD
2	Halleck	ARENDS	A	H	A^a	A	A	A	A	A
3	Arends			A						
No. of departures: 3										
SD 1	Barkley	L	McFarland	J	J	J	J	M	M	M
2	Lucas	Myers	Johnson	Clements	C	Mansfield	M	Humphrey	H	Long
No. of departures: 0										
SR 1	White	W	W	TAFT	KNOWLAND	K	D	D	D	D
2	Wherry	Saltonstall	S	S	S	DIRKSEN	Kuchel	K	K	K
No. of departures: 3										

Initials represent a repetition of the name; e.g., R = Rayburn.
Names in small capitals indicate departures from precedent; see text.
a. The change between the 83rd and 84th Congresses as a result of the Republican party's return to minority party status is a repetition of the change between the 80th and 81st. Arends remains as Whip throughout. Martin remains as top Republican leader. The "squeezing out" of Halleck as the number of Republican leadership positions is compressed from three to two has been designated as one "departure." See commentary in text.

98

50) through the 89th (1965–66) as providing opportunity for sixty-seven of the two kinds of departure listed above (not counting appointment of new Whips, but counting reappointment of Whips), one finds that only six of the cases—all occurring in the Republican party—could under the most generous estimate be called actual departures from the rule. The three occasions for Senate Republicans involve promotions to the position of Floor Leader over Saltonstall, who held the Whip position. And there is no evidence that Saltonstall, who was approaching retirement, wanted the job of Floor Leader. One instance for the House Republicans merely involved a reduction of the number of leadership posts caused by a change to minority party status. In 1949 and 1955, as the Democrats organized the House, Speaker Martin had to step down to become Minority Leader and Floor Leader Halleck was temporarily removed from leadership, while Arends remained Whip. Since if the hierarchy we are assuming here were strictly followed, Halleck, not Arends, would have become Whip, this has been counted as one departure from the rule. Actually the only two clear-cut cases involved Halleck's election as Minority Leader over Martin in 1959 and Ford's election over Halleck in 1965. Even counting all six, however, in only 9 per cent of the cases was there a deviation from the regular succession of posts. Party leaders, like committee leaders, are recruited through a stable, predictable series of subaltern posts. The procedure is somewhat less automatic than the selection of chairmen, but the processes are essentially similar.

Some instances of challenge and overthrow do occur, but they are the exception. In the 86th Congress, House Republicans defeated Minority Leader Martin and elected Charles Halleck to the post. But the Halleck leadership lasted only six years. After the 1964 election, a similar process was repeated, this time with Halleck losing out to Gerald R. Ford, Jr. These are the only two cases of sucessful challenge in recent House history. Both occurred in the minority party and after particularly severe party losses in the preceding election, leading some to conclude that minority party frustrations may be a catalyst for revolt.[7] After the 1968 election, House Democratic liberals tried to unseat Speaker McCormack. But the Udall challenge failed by the decisive margin of 178–58, provoking one disappointed liberal to remark, "I don't think we can change this place."[8]

The stability in office and in apprenticeship for both groups is at least partially explainable in terms of the underlying stability of congressional membership. The low turnover of congressmen has led to the growth of stable, fairly automatic procedures for selecting leaders.[9] And it can be shown decade by decade from 1890 to 1963 that as House membership became more stable, the seniority rule grew stronger.[10] The Senate, with a more stable membership in the nineteenth century than the House, had adopted an automatic seniority rule back in the nineteenth century. In other words, seniority tends to be supported by a stable congressional membership,[11] while a consistently "junior" membership, characterized by frequent turnover, would have little use for a seniority rule.

Constituency Characteristics and Policy

To WHAT EXTENT DO PARTY LEADERS AND COMMITtee leaders have similar constituencies and policy leanings? As Table 27 shows, party leaders seem to hold even safer seats than committee leaders. The records of the four congressional parties closely parallel each other. Senate Republican party leaders included four members whose division of the vote in their districts averaged less than 60 per cent, while Senate Republican committee leaders averaged a more "competitive" 57.2 per cent. House Republican party and committee leaders averaged 60.8 and 61.9 per cent, respectively. Senate Democrats are also similar—69.5 per cent for committee leaders compared to 64.7 per cent for party leaders. Actually for 14 of these 20 years, the party was led by Lyndon Johnson and Mike

Mansfield, who averaged 76.0 and 70.4 per cent of the vote, respectively. At the extreme in safeness, House Democratic committee leaders averaged 79.4 per cent, but the party leaders —Rayburn, McCormack, and Albert—top them all with a mean percentage of 91.6 per cent.

Other similarities can be noted. Party leaders and committee leaders resemble each other in the types of state or district they represent. Chapter IV revealed that in the House, the largest concentration of Democratic committee leaders came from rural districts, and the largest concentration of Republican committee leaders from midurban districts; much the same is true of party leaders. Senate Republican party leaders, like the party's committee leaders, tend to come from the states of largest population (first quartile). Along regional lines, the two groups of Republican leaders both tend to be drawn from the Midwest or the East. Democrats tend to be drawn from the South, which supplied two of the three House leaders and two of the five Senate leaders.

On policy, however, the two groups differ. In recent American politics, party leaders have come to be considered the President's lieutenants in Congress. They have strong congressional ties of their own which may produce a kind of ambivalence as they try to perform at once the role of congressional leader and that of presidential aide. But their jobs and their prestige are closely linked to the legislative success of the President's program (assuming the White House and Congress are controlled by the same party). Therefore it is not surprising to find, among party leaders, a record of strong support of President and party, expressed not only in roll-call votes but in active championship. All available data show scores for party leaders at least as high, and sometimes higher than those of congressional party members, in support of President and party on roll-call votes.[12] In seven of the eight cases moderately high support scores had been in evidence well before the congressmen had gained a position of leadership. Only Hale Boggs of Louisiana showed a substantial increase in support of the party

Table 27. Constituency Characteristics of Party Leaders, 1947–66[a]

	Number of Terms Served 1947–66	Region	Mean Per Cent of Total Vote in District 1947–66[a]	Type of Congressional District	State Population Quartile Rank
Senate Democrats					
A. Barkley, Kentucky	1	South	54.8		2nd
S. Lucas, Illinois	1	Midwest	52.6		1st
E. McFarland, Arizona	1	West	69.7		4th
L. Johnson, Texas	4	South	76.0		1st
M. Mansfield, Montana	3	West	70.4		4th
			Mean = 64.7		
House Democrats					
S. Rayburn, Texas	7.5	South	99.2	Rural	
J. McCormack, Mass.	8	East	91.1	Urban	
C. Albert, Oklahoma	3	South	84.6	Rural	
			Mean = 91.6		

TABLE 27.—cont.

	Number of Terms Served 1947–66	Region	Mean Per Cent of Total Vote in District 1947–66a	Type of Congressional District	State Population Quartile Rank
Senate Republicans					
W. White, Maine	1	East	66.6		3rd
K. Wherry, Nebraska	1	Midwest	56.7		3rd
S. Bridges, N. H.	0.5	East	58.5		4th
R. Taft, Ohio	0.5	Midwest	57.5		1st
W. Knowland, Cal.	2.5	West	100.0		1st
E. Dirksen, Illinois	4	Midwest	53.6		1st
			Mean=65.5		
House Republicans					
C. Halleck, Indiana	5	Midwest	58.4	Rural	
J. Martin, Jr., Mass.	6	East	62.8	Midurban	
G. Ford, Michigan	1	Midwest	61.2	Midurban	
			Mean=60.8		

a. The number of terms analyzed is limited to the years 1947–66 in order to make the analysis for party leaders comparable to the earlier analyses for committee leaders and members. Thus five party leaders had served a larger number of terms and had begun their service at an earlier age than the above numbers indicate. These five include Sam Rayburn, John McCormack, Joseph Martin, Jr., Alben Barkley, and Wallace White. A "term" refers to the two-year span of each Congress.

Vote totals were counted only for those elections immediately preceding the congressman's term as party leader. Thus for Senators the election counted may have occurred from zero to four years before the term as party leader.

District and state population categories follow the classification used in earlier sections of the book. States in the first quartile of population include the twelve states with largest populations, and so on.

after he became Majority Whip.[13] This and earlier studies lead to the same conclusion: "The recruitment of party leaders favored 'moderates' in both parties."[14]

Despite these differences in policy between party and committee leaders, numerous instances of mutual accommodation and support can be cited. Of particular interest are those questions of "seniority" and "reform" which touch their shared vested interest in the congressional institution. For example, although by 1962 Majority Leader McCormack had accumulated some unpopularity among both Southerners and Democratic Study Group liberals, his election to the Speakership was not contested. One key reason cited was that McCormack received the support of two powerful House chairmen—Vinson and Smith.[15] A more detailed illustration of mutual accommodation and consultation between these two groups of senior leaders is provided by Speaker Rayburn's long-awaited acquiescence in the 87th Congress to the plan to expand the Rules Committee.[16]

Democratic Study Group liberals had been negotiating with Rayburn since the 86th Congress to "do something" about the Rules Committee, notorious for its bottling up of liberal legislation through its combined conservative Democratic and Republican majority. At first Rayburn did nothing. He had an agreement, he said, with the Republican leaders not to change the size of Rules nor the eight-to-four majority-minority ratio. After the 1960 election the issue was raised again. Four Mississippi Democrats—William Colmer, John Bell Williams, Arthur Winstead, and Jamie Whitten—had deserted the Democratic candidate for President to support an unpledged slate of presidential electors. A fifth maverick, Louisiana's Otto Passman, also refused to back Kennedy, although he did not announce support of Nixon. The liberal position at the start of the 87th Congress was that the party caucus should punish these five by stripping them of their seniority and their committee seats. Colmer, second-ranking member on Rules, was the key target. His politics have been described by Representative

Richard Bolling as "perhaps slightly to the left of Ivan the Terrible."[17] The proposed party discipline would remove Colmer from the Rules Committee and replace him with a moderate.

Rayburn did not agree to the liberal proposal. He did agree, however, to try for an enlargement of the committee, which would give the liberals a tenuous eight-to-seven majority, but would allow the five threatened conservatives to keep their committee seniority. Before this decision, he discussed the matter with committee chairman Vinson and received his support for enlargement. Rayburn also consulted with Howard Smith, Chairman of Rules. Bolling reports that throughout the days preceding the Rules fight, "messages shuttled back and forth between Rayburn and Smith."[18] Smith agreed to report out the resolution for enlargement, although he reserved the right to vote against it. Despite the severe differences between Rayburn and Smith on the issue, the existence of this consultation and communication deserves underlining. And the nature of Rayburn's decision itself merits further comment. Liberal Democratic Senator Clark remarks on Rayburn's decision not to remove Colmer:

That would have constituted a crime against the Establishment, which places far more emphasis on the prerogatives and traditions of the Congress as an institution than it does on a Presidential program. To remove Colmer would have meant tampering with seniority . . . risking a rupture with the Southern wing of the Party.[19]

Speaker Rayburn's decision can thus be seen as a compromise which supported neither faction, but was not wholly unsatisfactory to either. The decision was taken after consultation with key committee chairmen. It was an excellent example of a senior party leader's support of the principle of seniority.

For another, briefer example from the Senate, consider Joseph Clark's attempt in 1963 to make the Democratic Steering Committee more geographically and ideologically representative by increasing the size of the committee. In effect, he wanted more Northern liberal Democrats on the committee. But for this change, he needed the support of the Senate Democratic leadership, which happened to consist of two Northern Democrats —Majority Leader Mansfield of Montana and Democratic Whip Humphrey of Minnesota. Clark reported that, to his surprise, Mansfield opposed his motion, and Humphrey failed to support it. The motion lost. Clark summarizes—somewhat unnecessarily perhaps—"Had the Majority Leader and Whip supported Senator Anderson and me, I believe we would have won."[20]

Patterns of mutual support between these leaders deserve further study, but the examples above suggest considerable reciprocal support on organizational and reform issues—a dimension not tapped by the traditional roll-call studies.

Summary

DESPITE DIFFERENT FORMAL MODES OF SELECTION, the congressional careers of both party and committee leaders appear similar in length of prior service, existence of apprenticeship posts, the security that comes from the stability and predictability of the process of selection, and a common dependence on seniority norms. Both groups tend to hold safe seats and to represent similar types of constituency. But they differ in recorded policy stands, particularly as regards support of party and President. Indeed, the widely noted "pivotal" position of party leaders may reflect the combined similarities and differences between the two groups. Hence one might not expect party leaders enthusiastically to support proposals like that of Representative Bolling, described at the beginning of the chapter, even though such schemes purport to increase their power. At the very least, both kinds of leaders have lived together long enough in Congress to have developed habits of consultation and mutual accommodation. But also their common dependence on the norm of seniority may help explain support by party leaders for the system of selection that gives power to their senior colleagues.

VIII

The Seniority System and the Congress

IT SHOULD NOW BE POSSIBLE to advance further generalizations about the seniority system as a device for selecting leaders in Congress. We shall consider first its effects on the kind of leaders selected; and second, its place in the larger pattern of Congressional action.

The Impact of the Seniority System

PERHAPS THE SINGLE MOST IMPORTANT FINDING OF this study is that the effect of the seniority system on the kind of committee chairmen selected by congress is at most a limited one. Democratic committee chairmen or ranking minority members, taken as a group, reflect with fair accuracy the composition of the Democratic members in Congress, and the Republican leaders even more accurately reflect their party's membership. Thus Southerners have filled more than 50 per cent of the Democratic committee chairs in the past two decades, and Southerners have usually comprised more than 50 per cent of the Democratic membership of the House and Senate.

The effect of the seniority system is limited because its requirement of continuous service in House or Senate can be met by a majority of congressmen. The majority of House and Senate seats are safe for the incumbents. Indeed, there are more

congressmen qualified by long congressional service for committee chairs than there are chairs to be filled; hence factors
other than congressional seniority, such as original committee
assignments, and subsequent reassignments, can and do influence the selection of chairmen.

While the seniority system reflects the distribution of members, the reflection may be subject to some distortion. The
congressional seniority requirement does screen out the small
number of states and districts which switch party frequently.
And at times of majority party upsets, the committee leadership
may in the short run, be noticeably unrepresentative of Congress as a whole. Thus the increase of Midwestern strength in the
congressional Democratic parties since the late 1950's has only
recently begun to show up in the geographical redistribution
of chairmanships. Because of this time lag, the seniority links
congressional leadership not to the party as it is but to the party
as it used to be. Actually, the difference is usually not large
because of the stability of voting preferences.

The seniority system also provides a magnifying effect: it
gives a bonus to the majority faction in the party, whether
majorities are reckoned on a basis of North versus South, rural
versus urban, or liberal versus conservative. Critics have
stressed that the seniority system benefits those kinds of congressmen who have been in office longest. But in practice, the
group with the longest tenure has tended also to be the largest
and strongest group. The present analysis has shown that the
group, geographical or other, with the largest number of members of Congress nearly always turns out to have the largest
number of chairmanships (or ranking minority members). The
one exception is the overrepresentation of rural districts among
House Democrats.

Since the effects of congressional seniority on the selection
of chairmen are marginal at most, the seniority system permits
considerable variation in the way chairmanships are distributed.
Republicans, but not Democrats, exhibit an extremely close fit
between leaders and all members of the congressional party.

The degree of unrepresentativeness within the parties also varies. This suggests that factors other than length of congressional service, such as patterns of committee assignments and reassignment, might be studied further for their influence on the selection of chairmen.

On the basis of these findings, it may be interesting to reconsider the traditional criticism of the seniority rule.

Basically, there is no evidence that application of this rule results in regional bias. The geographical distribution of the members of Congress is reproduced in the leaders on a regional and even more clearly on a state-by-state basis. Some advantage in Democratic chairmanships accrues to both the South and the West. Congressional seniority can help to explain Southern, but not Western, overrepresentation.

Democratic members from rural districts are overrepresented by committee chairmen and those from all other districts (not merely metropolitan districts) are underrepresented. But this is not true of Republicans. The rural overrepresentation among Democratic chairmen cannot be explained by the congressional seniority requirement, nor fully explained by rural-urban differences in committee changes. While committee seniority appears to play some part in benefiting the rural congressmen, again the luck or discretion involved in original committee assignments may influence the results.

Nor are small states (by population) overrepresented in the Senate. No systematic misrepresentation of states by population is observable for either party.

As to policy stands, Democratic committee chairmen show some conservative bias, and some bias against support for their party or President; Republicans do not. The Republican committee leaders followed almost exactly the same pattern as all Republican members of Congress in roll-call voting. The leaders were no more conservative than the Republican membership. The bias for conservatism and against party and President is found among Northern as well as Southern Democrats. While these effects are traceable in part to the congressional seniority requirement, all stages in the process of selecting chairmen—congressional seniority, original committee assignments, committee changes—appeared to contribute to the conservative cast of the Democratic chairmen.

The Seniority System and the Congress

How does the seniority rule affect the operation of Congress? Congress differs from many other organizations in that it does not control the selection of its own members. Members of Congress are elected by the voters. The seniority rule, then, provides a key organizational link between the party system and Congress and between the members of Congress and its leaders. Under the system, leaders are chosen from among the senior members, those who know well the organization's rules and customs. And they are chosen in a way that reinforces the main areas of strength, the established interests in the majority party in Congress. The process reflects fairly accurately the composition of the party in Congress as it has been formed over time. Where it distorts, it does so by giving the majority faction in the congressional party an increased advantage. It thus reinforces traditional areas of party strength. It helps the political parties to organize the Congress in a way that ensures that established *party* interests and established *congressional* interests will not conflict, and in a way that strengthens them both.

The seniority rule rewards age and continuous service in a body that prides itself on its long traditions and continuity. The average age in Congress is the highest in any major Western legislature.[1] The seniority rule builds a time lag into the selection of leaders of a body well known for other time lags. It gives some slight advantage to intraparty groups and factions in Congress that were already strong, and usually already dominant, in the membership. Hence, when bills are obstructed in committee, there is often reason to believe that if reported

111

out, they would be obstructed on the floor. Graham Barden, foe of federal aid to education, used every obstructionist device available to a chairman and some improvisations of his own to stop aid bills in committee. After Barden's retirement and the elevation of liberal Adam Clayton Powell to the chairmanship of House Education and Labor, aid to education bills were stopped by the Rules Committee or defeated on the floor. The seniority system reflects and reinforces a deeper congressional conservatism.

Moreover, it helps to reinforce the decentralized character of leadership in Congress, which protects the diverse interests of the members and strengthens Congress's independence of the Presidency. Power centralized in the hands of party leaders could be more easily controlled from the outside than power dispersed among many centers. The seniority system helps Congress to defend itself against outside control by preventing lines of influence from forming between Congress and the White House. It strengthens the Congress in its well-known desire to be independent of the Presidency. As Roger Davidson and colleagues remark:

The influence of Congress is enhanced . . . because seniority leaders represent "immovable" objects with which the executive branch must contend. . . . Many members who are troubled over the decline of Congress take comfort from the belief that, however irksome a chairman may seem to his colleagues, he may be even more so to executive-branch officials.[2]

The seniority system clearly strengthens the particularistic, centrifugal tendencies in the Congress. By multiplying centers of power down to the level of committee chairmen, it contributes to the fragmentation of power which frequently makes any attempt to form a governing majority impossible.

Finally, and crucially important in a Congress which is characterized by plural, decentralized leadership and multiple interests, and in which the political process requires the forming and reforming of coalitions, the seniority system offers stability in the distribution of influence. It offers *predictability* concerning who has power in what area. Such predictability would seem a necessary prerequisite for carrying on political business. Thus the seniority system offers something valuable to leaders—both party and committee leaders—and members alike, as well as to interested parties outside Congress.

One of the most intriguing phenomena in the study of political institutions is the way systems perpetuate themselves, create and nourish subsystems that reinforce the parent system. Both leaders and ordinary members of Congress are attached to the seniority system because they profit by the stability, predictability, and maintenance of traditional power alignments which it fosters. And by contributing this stability, predictability, and support of decentralized leadership, the seniority system helps to support the larger congressional system which has produced and is nourishing it.

An exception to these remarks are, of course, the opponents of the system, who constitute a small minority of congressmen, supported by some outsiders. But these opponents seek change. They seek a more centralized distribution of influence in Congress which would be more sensitive to presidential leadership, not tendencies reinforcing decentralization and congressional independence. These opponents clearly seek a different kind of Congress, which, in view of the stable, mutually reinforcing tendencies described above, will not easily be effected. Indeed, the present study suggests that if change *is* to be effected, it will come not through altering the seniority rule or defeating Speakers of the House, but through gradual changes in the membership of Congress, brought about by the voters in elections.

For in one sense, the critics are quite correct. The seniority system is a profoundly conservative institution—not because it biases the kind of leaders selected, but because it reinforces the conservatism already present in Congress.

Bibliography

Notes

Index

Selected Bibliography

THE MAJOR SOURCES FOR THIS STUDY are the following reference books supplying data on members of Congress and their constituencies: *Official Congressional Directory* (Washington, D.C.: Government Printing Office, the first edition for each Congress, 1921–1966); *Congress and the Nation: 1945–1964* (Washington, D.C.: Congressional Quarterly Service, 1965); *America Votes* (Washington: Congressional Quarterly, Inc.), vols. I–VI; and U.S. Bureau of the Census, *Congressional District Data Book (Districts of the 88th Congress)*—A Statistical Abstract Supplement (Washington, D.C.: Government Printing Office, 1963).

A highly selective list of relevant sources is given below, categorized by kind of study: (1) historical studies of the seniority system and related studies of Congress; (2) the reform commentary; and (3) other recent relevant studies of Congress.

Historical Studies

Abram, Michael, and Joseph Cooper, "The Rise of Seniority in the House of Representatives," *Polity*, Fall, 1968, pp 52–85.

Alexander, DeAlva Stanwood, *History and Procedure of the House of Representatives*, Boston, Houghton Mifflin, 1916.

Berdahl, Clarence A., "Some Notes on Party Membership in Congress," I–III, *American Political Science Review*, April, June, August, 1949.

Chamberlain, Joseph P., *Legislative Processes: National and State*, New York, Appleton-Century, 1936.

Donovan, Robert J., *Eisenhower: The Inside Story*, New York, Harper, 1956.

Eisenhower, Dwight D., *The White House Years: Mandate for Change, 1953–56*, New York, Doubleday, 1963.

Freidel, Frank, *F. D. R. and the South*, Baton Rouge, Louisiana State University Press, 1965.

Galloway, George B., *History of the House of Representatives*, New York, Crowell, 1961.

Haynes, George H., *The Senate of the United States*, 2 vols., New York, Russell & Russell, 1938.

Hughes, Emmet John, *The Ordeal of Power*, New York, Atheneum, 1963.

Ickes, Harold L., *The Secret Diary of Harold L. Ickes: The First Thousand Days, 1933–1936*, New York, Simon and Schuster, 1953.

Luce, Robert, *Congress: An Explanation*, Cambridge, Harvard University Press, 1926.

MacNeil, Neil, *Forge of Democracy*, New York, McKay, 1963.

Martin, Joe, *My First Fifty Years in Politics*, New York, McGraw-Hill, 1960.

Mayer, George H., *The Republican Party, 1854–1966*, 2nd ed., New York, Oxford University Press, 1967.

McConachie, Lauros Grant, *Congressional Committees*, New York, Crowell, 1898.

Patterson, James T., *Congressional Conservatism and the New Deal*, Lexington, University of Kentucky Press, 1967.

Perkins, Frances, *The Roosevelt I Knew*, New York, Viking, 1946.

Pollock, James K., Jr., "Seniority Rule in Congress," *North American Review*, CCXXII (December, 1925), 235–245.

Polsby, Nelson W., Miriam Gallagher, and Barry Spencer Rundquist, "The Growth of the Seniority System in the U.S. House of Representatives," American Political Science Association paper, Washington, D.C., September, 1968.

Price, Charles, and Joseph Boskin, "The Roosevelt 'Purge'; A Reappraisal," *Journal of Politics*, XXVIII (August, 1966), 660–670.

Ripley, Randall B., "The Development of Party Leadership in the United States Senate," unpublished draft.

Rossiter, Clinton, "President and Congress in the 1960's," in *Continuing Crisis in American Politics*, ed. Marian Irish, Englewood Cliffs, N.J., Prentice-Hall, 1963.

Rovere, Richard H., *The Eisenhower Years*, New York, Farrar, Straus & Cudahy, 1956.

Schlesinger, Arthur M., Jr., *The Age of Roosevelt: The Crisis of the Old Order*, vol. I, Boston, Houghton Mifflin, 1957.

Shannon, J. B., "Presidential Politics in the South: 1938," *Journal of Politics*, May and August, 1939, pp. 146–170, 278–300.

Tugwell, Rexford G., *The Democratic Roosevelt*, New York, Doubleday, 1957.

Reform Commentary

American Political Science Association, *The Reorganization of Congress*, American Political Science Association, 1945.

Bolling, Richard, *House Out of Order*, New York, Dutton, 1965.

Brewer, F. M., "Chairmanships in Congress," *Editorial Research Reports*, vol. II, 1947.

Burns, James MacGregor, *Congress on Trial*, New York, Harper, 1949.

———, *The Deadlock of Democracy*, Englewood Cliffs, N.J., Prentice-Hall, 1963.

Celler, Emanuel, "The Seniority Rule in Congress," *Western Political Quarterly*, March, 1961, pp. 160–167.

Clark, Joseph S., *Congress: The Sapless Branch*, rev. ed., New York, Harper & Row, 1964.

———, ed., *Congressional Reform: Problems and Prospects*, New York, Crowell, 1965.

Congressional Quarterly, "Congressional Reform," *CQ Special Report*, June 7, 1963.

Galloway, George B., *Congress at the Crossroads*, New York, Crowell, 1946.

———, *History of the House of Representatives*, New York, Crowell, 1961.

Heller, Robert, *Strengthening the Congress*, Washington, D.C., National Planning Association, 1945.

Krock, Arthur, "The Lords Proprietors of Congress," *New York Times Magazine*, January 22, 1967, pp. 28ff.

Lindsay, John V., "The Seniority System," in *We Propose: A Modern Congress*, proposals by House Republican Task Force on Congressional Reform and Minority Staffing, New York, McGraw-Hill, 1966.

Udall, Stewart L., "A Defense of the Seniority System," *New York Times Magazine*, January 13, 1957.

U.S. Congress, Joint Committee on the Organization of Congress, *Second Interim Report*, 89th Cong., 2nd Sess., Senate Report 948, January, 1966.

———, *Hearings*, Part 1. 79th Cong., 1st Sess., March, 1945.

———, Senate Special Committee on the Organization of Congress, *Hearings*, 89th Cong., 2nd Sess., 1966.

Young, Roland, *The American Congress*, New York, Harper, 1958.

Recent Relevant Studies

Abram, Michael, and Joseph Cooper, "The Rise of Seniority in the House of Representatives," *Polity*, Fall, 1968, pp. 52–85.

Campbell, Angus, Philip E. Converse, Warren E. Miller, and Donald E. Stokes, *Elections and the Political Order*, New York, Wiley, 1960.

Clapp, Charles L., *The Congressman: His Work as He Sees It*, New York, Doubleday, 1963.

Cummings, Milton C., Jr., and Robert L. Peabody, "The Decision to Enlarge the Committee on Rules . . . ," in *New Perspectives on the House of Representatives*, ed. Robert L. Peabody and Nelson W. Polsby, Chicago, Rand McNally, 1963.

Davidson, Roger H., David M. Kovenock, and Michael K. O'Leary, *Congress in Crisis: Politics and Congressional Reform*, Belmont, Calif., Wadsworth Publishing Co., 1966.

Fenno, Richard F., Jr., "The House Appropriations Committee as a Political System," *American Political Science Review*, June, 1962, pp. 310–324.

————, "The Internal Distribution of Influence: The House," in *Congress and America's Future*, ed. David B. Truman, Englewood Cliffs, N.J., Prentice-Hall, 1965.

Froman, Lewis A., Jr., *The Congressional Process: Strategies, Rules, and Procedures*, Boston, Little, Brown, 1967.

————, and Randall Ripley, "Conditions for Party Leadership: The Case of the House Democrats," *American Political Science Review*, March, 1965, pp. 52–63.

Goodwin, George, Jr., "The Seniority System in Congress," *American Political Science Review*, June, 1959, pp. 412–436.

Griffith, Ernest S., *Congress: Its Contemporary Role*, 4th ed., New York, New York University Press, 1967.

Hacker, Andrew, *Congressional Districting*, rev. ed., Washington, D.C., Brookings Institution, 1964.

Hinckley, Barbara, "Congressional Elections Research: Some Beginnings," paper delivered at the Annual Meeting of the American Political Science Association, New York, September, 1969.

Huitt, Ralph K., "The Congressional Committee: A Case Study," *American Political Science Review*, June, 1954, pp 340–365.

————, "Democratic Party Leadership in the Senate," *American Political Science Review*, June, 1961, pp. 333–344.

————, "The Morse Committee Assignment Controversy: A Study in Senate Norms," *American Political Science Review*, June, 1957, pp. 313–329.

Jones, Charles O., "Inter-Party Competition for Congressional Seats," *Western Political Quarterly*, September, 1964, pp. 461–476.

————, "Joseph G. Cannon and Howard W. Smith; An Essay on the Limits of Leadership in the House of Representatives," *Journal of Politics*, August, 1968, pp 617–646.

Manley, John F., "Wilbur D. Mills," paper presented at the Annual Meeting of the American Political Science Association, Washington, D.C., September, 1968.

Marwell, Gerald, "Party, Region and the Dimensions of Conflict in the House of Representatives, 1949–1954," *American Political Science Review*, June, 1967, pp. 380–399.

Masters, Nicholas A., "Committee Assignments in the House of Representatives," *American Political Science Review*, June, 1961, pp. 345–357.

Matthews, Donald R., *U.S. Senators and Their World*, New York, Vintage, 1960.

Miller, Warren E., and Donald E. Stokes, *Representation in the American Congress*, forthcoming.

Peabody, Robert L., "Party Leadership Change in the House of Representatives," *American Political Science Review*, September, 1967, pp. 675–693.

Pennock, J. Roland, and John W. Chapman, eds., *Representation: Nomos X*, New York, Atherton Press, 1968.

Pfeiffer, David G., "The Measurement of Inter-Party Competition and Systemic Stability," *American Political Science Review*, June, 1967, pp. 457–467.

Pitkin, Hanna Fenichel, *The Concept of Representation*, Berkeley, University of California Press, 1967.

Polsby, Nelson W., "The Institutionalization of the U.S. House of Representatives," *American Political Science Review*, March, 1968, pp. 144–168.

————, Miriam Gallagher, and Barry Spencer Rundquist, "The Growth of the Seniority System in the U.S. House of Representatives," American Political Science Association paper, Washington, D.C., September, 1968.

Ripley, Randall, *Party Leaders in the House of Representatives*, Washington, D.C., Brookings Institution, 1967.

Schlesinger, Joseph A., *Ambition and Politics*, Chicago, Rand McNally, 1966.

Truman, David B., *The Congressional Party*, New York, Wiley, 1959.

Wolfinger, Raymond E., and Joan Heifetz, "Safe Seats, Seniority and Power in Congress," *American Political Science Review*, June, 1965, pp. 337–349.

Notes

1. The Seniority System: An Introduction

1. Emanuel Celler, "The Seniority Rule in Congress," *Western Political Quarterly*, XIV (March, 1961), 160. See also Ernest S. Griffith, *Congress: Its Contemporary Role* (4th ed., New York, New York University Press, 1967), 31.

2. Preliminary studies include George Goodwin, "The Seniority System in Congress," *American Political Science Review*, June, 1959, pp. 412–417; Donald R. Matthews, *U.S. Senators and Their World* (New York, Vintage, 1960), pp. 147–175. A work in progress by Milton Cummings, Jr., should be helpful. For the history of the seniority system, see Nelson W. Polsby, Miriam Gallagher, and Barry Spencer Rundquist, "The Growth of the Seniority System in the U.S. House of Representatives," paper presented at the American Political Science Association meeting, September, 1968, Washington, D.C.; and Michael Abram and Joseph Cooper, "The Rise of Seniority in the House of Representatives," *Polity*, Fall, 1968, 52–85.

3. For a sample of the criticism, see Roland Young, *The American Congress* (New York, Harper, 1958), p. 108; George Galloway, *Congress at the Crossroads* (New York, Crowell, 1946), pp. 127–145; Joseph Clark, *Congress: The Sapless Branch* (rev. ed., New York, Harper & Row, 1964), p. 178; and James MacGregor Burns, *The Deadlock of Democracy* (Englewood Cliffs, N.J., Prentice-Hall, 1963), p. 244. Note also Arthur M. Schlesinger's comment on the difficulties President Kennedy faced with a Congress run by the seniority system: "The legislative process of the New Frontier was thus largely in the hands of aging men, mostly born in another century, mostly representing rural areas in an urban nation." *A Thousand Days* (Boston, Houghton Mifflin, 1965), p. 709

4. See for example *Congressional Quarterly Special Report,* April, 1964, p. 18; Matthews, pp. 163–165; James MacGregor Burns, *Congress on Trial* (New York, Harper & Row, 1949), p. 134; Stephen K. Bailey, *The New Congress* (New York, St. Martin's Press, 1966), p. 57.

5. See for example Burns, *Congress on Trial,* p. 134; Griffith, p. 32; Bailey, p. 57; Douglass Cater, *Power in Washington* (New York, Random House, 1964), pp. 144–160.

6. Matthews, pp. 163–165; Clark, p. 177; *Congressional Quarterly Special Report,* June 7, 1963, p. 878; *New York Times,* editorial, "The Tyranny of Seniority," July 15, 1966, p. 30.

7. Galloway, pp. 189, 190; Celler, p. 190; Young, p. 110; Griffith, p. 34. Charles Clapp calls this the congressmen's characteristic defense of the system: *The Congressman: His Work as He Sees It* (New York, Harper, 1963), p. 257.

8. U.S. Congress, Joint Committee on the Organization of Congress, *Second Interim Report,* S. Rept. 948 (1965), pp. 7, 8.

9. See for example Burns, *Congress on Trial,* pp. 58, 59; and *Congressional Quarterly Weekly Report,* June 7, 1963, pp. 877, 878.

10. U.S. Congress, Joint Committee on the Organization of Congress, 89th Congress, 1st Session, 1965, *Hearings,* Part 1, pp. 132–165.

11. Clarence A. Berdahl "Some Notes on Party Membership in Congress: Part II," *American Political Science Review,* June, 1949, pp. 492–508; Ralph K. Huitt, "The Morse Committee Assignment Controversy: A Study in Senate Norms," *American Political Science Review,* June, 1957, pp. 319, 320.

12. Huitt, "Morse Committee," pp. 313–329.

13. See Polsby et al.; also Randall B. Ripley, "The Development of Party Leadership in the United States Senate," unpublished draft, for documentation of the point that recent violations of seniority in House and Senate are virtually nil.

14. Richard Fenno, Jr. "The Internal Distribution of Influence: The House," in *The Congress and America's Future,* ed. David B. Truman (Englewood Cliffs, N.J., Prentice-Hall, 1965), pp. 52–76.

15. See Polsby et al., pp. 26, 27; Ripley; and Abrams and Cooper, p. 81.

16. Ripley, pp. 21–24.

17. Polsby et al., p. 27.

18. Neil MacNeil, *Forge of Democracy* (New York, David McKay, 1963), pp. 123, 124.

19. Woodrow Wilson, *Constitutional Government in the United States* (New York, Columbia University Press, 1961), orig. pub. 1908, pp. 137, 138.

20. See Nelson W. Polsby, "The Institutionalization of the House of Representatives," *American Political Science Review, March,* 1968, p. 146.

21. Richard Bolling, *House Out of Order* (New York, Dutton, 1965), p. 90.

22. Ibid.

23. Clark, *Congress: The Sapless Branch,* pp. 180, 181.

24. The standard sources are V. O. Key, Jr., *Politics, Parties, and Pressure Groups* (5th ed., New York, Crowell, 1964) and "A Theory of Critical Elections," *Journal of Politics,* February, 1955, pp. 3–18; Angus Campbell, Philip E. Converse, Warren E. Miller, and Donald E. Stokes, *The American Voter* (New York, Wiley, 1960), and *Elections and the Political Order* (New York, Wiley, 1966), esp. pp. 125–135.

25. Barbara Hinckley, "Congressional Elections Research: Some Beginnings," paper presented at the Annual Meeting of the American Political Science Association, New York, September, 1969.

26. Key, *Politics, Parties, and Pressure Groups;* see also Charles Press, "Voting Statistics and Presidential Coattails," *American Political Science Review,* December, 1958, 1041–1050; "Presidential Coattails and Party Cohesion," *Midwest Journal of Political Science,* November, 1963, pp. 320–325; and Barbara Hinckley, "Interpreting House Midterm Elections: Toward a Measurement of the In-Party's 'Expected' Loss of Seats," *American Political Science Review,* September, 1967, pp. 694–700.

27. See for example the analysis by Ralph K. Huitt, "The Congressional Committee: A Case Study," *American Political Science Review,* June, 1954, pp. 340–365; and Matthews, pp. 47–67.

28. The source for identification of committee leaders, seniors, and committee seniors is *Official Congressional Directory* (Washington, D.C., Government Printing Office). The first edition in which committee lists were supplied for each Congress, 1947–1966, was used.

29. Hanna Fenichel Pitkin refers to this as "descriptive representation." *The Concept of Representation* (Berkeley, Uninversity of California Press, 1967), pp. 60–91.

30. Senator Pugh, December 19, 1859, *Congressional Globe,* p. 178, cited by George Haynes, *The Senate of the United States* (New York, Russell & Russell, 1938), I, 298.

31. Lauros Grant McConachie, *Congressional Committees* (New York, Crowell, 1898), p. 326.

2. The Concept of "Seniority"

1. George Galloway, *Congress at the Crossroads* (New York, Crowell, 1946), p. 190. See also Richard Bolling, *House Out of Order* (New York,

Dutton, 1965), p. 107. This average held fairly constant for each party and chamber throughout the twenty years.

2. Infrequent exceptions to the overall pattern can be noted: median age of Senate Democrats climbed once into the seventies (1953–54); Senate Republicans dropped into the fifties (1947–52); and House Republicans dropped once into the fifties (1965–66). Each congressman's age was counted for each election.

3. Cf. George Goodwin, "The Seniority System in Congress," *American Political Science Review*, June, 1959, p. 420: "Chairmen are older . . . although perhaps not as markedly so as is commonly believed."

4. The mean was found to parallel the median closely. No trends toward shorter or longer initial service were evident through the time period. No significant regional variation was evident.

5. That the results are not influenced by variations in committee prestige can be shown by the committees where leaders exceeded this average. Among Senate Democrats, committees where leaders won more than two consecutive elections included: Agriculture, Appropriations, Armed Services, Banking and Currency (twice), Judiciary, Labor, Post Office, and Rules (twice). Among House Democrats: Appropriations (twice), Armed Services, Banking and Currency, Commerce (twice), Interior, Foreign Affairs (twice), Judiciary, Public Works (twice), Rules (twice), Science, Un-American Activities, and Ways and Means (three times). Ways and Means may be the only clear exception.

6. The mean number of years chairmen served before gaining top rank for each of the six levels of committees (high prestige to low) is as follows: for House Democrats, Rank I committees, 24.3; II, 15.3; III, 18.4; IV, 18.8; V, 10.7; VI, 7.0. For House Republicans, Rank I committees, 19.3; II, 16.0; III, 13.1; IV, 14.2; V, 9.5; VI, 14.4. Warren E. Miller and Donald E. Stokes, *Representation in the American Congress*, forthcoming.

7. Joseph A. Schlesinger, *Ambition and Politics* (Chicago, Rand McNally, 1966), p. 46.

8. The eleven major Senate committees and twelve major House committees of the period.

9. Raymond E. Wolfinger and Joan Heifetz, "Safe Seats, Seniority and Power in Congress," *American Political Science Review*, June, 1965, p. 346; Charles O. Jones, "Interparty Competition for Congressional Seats," *Western Political Quarterly*, September, 1964, pp. 461–476; V. O. Key, Jr., *Politics, Parties, and Political Pressure Groups* (5th ed., New York, Crowell, 1964), pp. 547, 558, 559; Julius Turner, "Primary Elections as the Alternative to Party Competition in 'Safe' Districts," Journal of Politics, 1953, pp. 197–199.

10. For purposes of comparison, the House can be considered on a statewide basis. Only fourteen states did not have at least three senior Representatives, and these were states of small population and thus disadvantaged in the House to start with—except, again, Connecticut.

11. Actually the Senate totals suggest less "competition" for committee leadership than the House totals do. There were 55 Senate Democratic seniors and 40 committee leaders; 51 Senate Republican seniors and 46 committee leaders.

3. Constituencies: By Geography

1. David R. Mayhew, *Party Loyalty Among Congressmen* (Cambridge, Harvard University Press, 1966), pp. 125–145.

2. For some documentation of the existence of regional blocs in the 91st to 83rd Congresses, see Gerald Marwell, "Party, Region, and the Dimensions of Conflict in the House of Representatives, 1949–1954," *American Political Science Review*, LXI (June, 1967), 380–399.

3. There is general agreement on state classification when a four-part scheme is used. See, for example, the usual *Congressional Quarterly* regional breakdowns, and Paul T. David, Ralph M. Goldman, and Richard C. Baine, *The Politics of National Party Conventions* (Washington, D.C., Brookings Institution, 1960). States are classified as follows: East includes Maine, New Hampshire, Vermont, Massachusetts, Connecticut, Rhode Island, New York, New Jersey, Delaware, Maryland, Pennsylvania, West Virginia; South includes Virginia, North Carolina, South Carolina, Georgia, Florida, Kentucky, Tennessee, Alabama, Mississippi, Arkansas, Louisiana, Oklahoma, Texas; Midwest includes Ohio, Michigan, Indiana, Illinois, Wisconsin, Minnesota, Iowa, Missouri, North Dakota, South Dakota, Nebraska, Kansas; West includes Montana, Idaho, Wyoming, Colorado, Utah, Nevada, New Mexico, Arizona, Washington, Oregon, California.

4. Chi square analysis supports the interparty difference. A chi square one-sample test can be used to test the similarity (one-to-one correspondence) between two distributions. It tests the hypothesis that two groups (here, members and committee leaders) differ significantly with respect to the relative frequency with which group members fall into various categories, and thus whether they can be considered to come from identical populations. Computation of chi square (X^2) yields a number which when interpreted by a chi square table gives the "level of significance" or measure of the significant difference in the distributions of the two populations. Thus, a level of significance of .05 means that there are only 5 chances in 100 that the difference in the two distributions can be attributed to chance.

Translated into terms of this paper, a chi square giving a level of significance of .05 or lower—.01—would mean that the differences between the regional distribution of all members and of the seniority members were great enough to be called statistically significant. One explanation of the logic, method, and application of the square technique can be found in Sidney Siegel, *Nonparametric Statistics for the Behavioral Sciences* (New York, McGraw-Hill, 1956), pp. 104–111, 174–179. For the chi square table, see p. 249. Discussion of chi square can be found in most statistics books.

As measured by chi square analysis, Republicans in both House and Senate showed more similarity between the distributions for leaders and members than the Democrats. For Senate Democrats, $X^2 = 15.6$; with three degrees of freedom, this is significant at the .01 level. In other words, the differences between the two distributions are statistically significant. For the Senate Republicans, $X^2 = 5.6$; with three degrees of freedom, this is not significant. In other words, one cannot reject the hypothesis that the differences are attributable to chance. For the House Democrats, $X^2 = 20.5$; with three degrees of freedom, significant at .01. For the House Republicans, $X^2 = 11.1$; at three degrees of freedom, significant at .05, but not at .01.

5. Joseph Clark, *Congress: The Sapless Branch* (rev. ed., New York, Harper & Row, 1964), p. 116.

6. Ibid., p. 179.

7. Raymond E. Wolfinger and Joan Heifetz, "Safe Seats, Security, and Power in Congress," *American Political Science Review*, June, 1965, p. 349.

8. The levels of overrepresentation of committee leaders compared to all members show this relationship quite clearly. Summing the difference in percentage points between committee leaders and members where percentages for committee leaders are larger than percentages for members, the index numbers for this overall unrepresentativeness are as follows: For the Democrats in 1921–32, Senate, 23; House, 25; for 1947–66, Senate, 23; House, 16. For the Republicans in 1921–32, Senate, 6; House, 8; for 1947–66, Senate, 10; House, 8.

9. Distributions for the regular seniors and the advanced seniors are both given to make clear that the stricter definition of seniority would not alter the findings in any significant way.

10. A committee senior is a "senior" congressman who (1) has stayed on one committee of initial appointment or (2), if elected before 1946 (before the Legislative Reorganization Act's condensation of committees and shuffling of assignments), has stayed on one committee assigned at the beginning of 1947.

11. In counting Senate elections, 1964 was omitted to make all states comparable in that each held six senatorial elections. Including 1964 would

have introduced a spurious factor into the relationship, since one-third of the states would have elected more Senators of one party—measured by absolute numbers or percentages—than the other simply by the fact that an additional election was added into the correlation. Further, of all the elections, that of 1964 would have the least influence on shaping the committee leadership for the 1947-66 period. But to be certain that the omission of 1964 did not in itself alter the results, I ran the same correlation with the addition of the 1964 election and found quite similar results. The correlation coefficient for the six elections in the Democratic party is .72; for the six elections plus 1964, .77. The correlation coefficient for the six elections in the Republican party is .77; for the six elections plus 1964, .78. Note that excluding the Southern states yielded a correlation coefficient of .71 between membership and leadership compared to .72 for all Senate Democrats.

12. Neither partial correlation is zero, for membership and committee leadership, controlling for the intervening effect of seniority (CA.B), or for seniority and committee leadership, controlling for the ancillary effect of membership (CB.A). For a good discussion of the logic and technique, see Hubert M. Blalock, *Social Statistics* (New York, McGraw-Hill, 1960), pp. 337–343, and Hayward R. Alker, Jr., *Mathematics and Politics* (New York: Macmillan, 1965), pp. 122–129. The partial correlation coefficients are as follows: $r(CA.B) = .24$ for Senate Democrats; .27 for Senate Republicans; $r(CB.A) = .29$ for Senate Democrats; .27 for Senate Republicans. The partial correlations are $r(CA.B) = .20$ for House Democrats, .53 for House Republicans; $r(CB.A) = .45$ for House Democrats, .25 for House Republicans.

13. State size has no direct bearing on committee leadership except through its influence on membership. The partial correlation between state size and committee leadership controlling for membership equals zero, for both House Democrats and Republicans. See Blalock, pp. 337–343.

14. Correlation coefficients between committee leadership and seniority defined as 3 consecutive elections won in the Senate, 9 for House Republicans, and 11 for House Democrats, are as follows: Senate Democrats, .78; Senate Republicans, .64; House Democrats, .86; and House Republicans, .93.

15. It might be added that this clustering in the House does not mask an underlying rural cast to the committee leadership from these states. The House leaders from these four states were not predominantly from rural or small-town districts. Of the nine Democratic chairmen whose districts could be classified by one of the *Congressional Quarterly* demographic classification schemes, five came from urban districts for a total two-party

proportion of almost 50 per cent urban. The remaining committee leaders came from districts either rural on the one hand or "suburban," "mid-urban," "small-town," or "mixed," the definitions varying with the classification scheme utilized. Designation of "urban" districts above at least serves to separate out those districts which were not rural or small-town. See *Congressional Quarterly Weekly Reports*, March 31, 1965; February 2, 1962; and August 21, 1964. See also Wolfinger and Heifetz, pp. 340, 346.

4. Constituencies: By Population Type

1. David R. Mayhew, *Party Loyalty among Congressmen* (Cambridge, Harvard University Press, 1966) p. 145.

2. Ibid., p. 81; see also Donald P. Matthews, *U.S. Senators and Their World* (New York, Vintage, 1960), p. 129.

3. Results of chi square analysis for states by population show that for Senate Democrats, $X^2 = 9.0$; at three degrees of freedom, significant at .05; for Senate Republicans, $X^2 = .8$, not significant.

4. For a similar point, a comparison of committee leaders and all congressmen for 1947–56 (based on state population according to the 1950 census) showed that in that decade the fourth-quartile states were over-represented among Democrats—27 to 19 per cent. This decade showed more Western than Southern overrepresentation and six of these twelve fourth-quartile states were Western.

5. *CQ Weekly Report*, March 30, 1956, pp. 360–363; February 2, 1962, pp. 153–169; and August 21, 1964, pp. 1784–1798.

6. *CQ* begins with the Bureau of the Census definition of "urban": a population center of 25,000 or more inhabitants. A congressional district is "urban" if a majority of its inhabitants live in communities at least this concentrated. *CQ* defines "rural" as all areas not designated as urban, and adds the following distinctions to discriminate degrees of population density. A rural district is one (a) at least two-thirds rural; or (b) one-half to two-thirds rural, with no city of 25,000 or more population. A small-town district is one (a) one-third to one-half urban and with a city of 25,000 to 50,000 or (b) more than one-half urban and with no city of 50,000 or more; or (c) one-third to one-half urban with a city of 50,000 or more, the city having less than one-third the total district population. A mid-urban district is one (a) more than one-half urban and with a city of 50,000 to 200,000; or (b) one-third to one-half urban and with a city of more than 50,000, the city having more than one-third the total district population; or (c) one-half to two-thirds urban and contains or is partly contained in a city of 200,000 or more. A metropolitan district is one more than two-thirds urban. *CQ Weekly Report*, March 30, 1956, p. 360.

7. *CQ Weekly Report,* August 21, 1964, p. 1784, classifies districts on the basis of their "predominant population group." Where 50 per cent or more of the population of a district lived in urban, suburban, or rural areas, these districts were designated by such terms. Districts where no such population concentration was found were designated "mixed." The definition of "suburban" follows the Census Bureau definition of "urban fringe" —closely settled areas contiguous to central cities, excluding fourteen urban areas with population over 100,000.

The modification is based on Andrew Hacker's classification scheme in *Congressional Districting* (rev. ed., Washington, D.C., Brookings Institution, 1964), pp. 90, 91. This classification limits rural districts to those where 90 per cent or more of the population live outside the areas designated urban by the Census Bureau. What this change does essentially is to remove a number of districts from *CQ's* rural category and place them in the mixed urban category, districts which would have been included in *CQ's* 1955–56 "small-town" category. These are districts which, according to Hacker, "have a life of their own" and cannot be "forced into an urban-suburban-rural trichotomy."

8. For House Democrats, $X^2 = 10.1$; 2 df, significant at .01. For House Republicans, $X^2 = 3.1$; not significant.

9. The distribution for Northern Democratic Representatives in the 88th Congress was rural, 15 per cent; mixed-urban, 29 per cent; suburban, 11 per cent; and urban, 45 per cent.

10. The median years' service for both groups was 18 years. The most senior members, with service extending from 20 through 38 years, included 7 rural and 5 urban Representatives. The least senior of these senior members, with service beginning in 1947, included 4 rural and 3 urban Representatives.

For a somewhat contradictory point, see Wolfinger and Heifetz, pp. 338–340; however, this is based on a dichotomous rural-urban classification scheme.

11. This greater tendency to committee-hopping among urban congressmen is supported by Raymond E. Wolfinger and Joan Heifetz, "Safe Seats, Security, and Power in Congress," *American Political Science Review,* June, 1965, p. 343.

5. Policy

1. Unfortunately, little evidence is available for individual committee chairmen. But for some pioneering work in the area, see John Bibby and Roger Davidson, "The Senate Committee on Banking and Currency," *On*

Capitol Hill (New York; Holt, Rinehart, and Winston, 1967), pp. 170–196; and John F. Manley, "Wilbur D. Mills," paper presented at the 1968 Annual Meeting of the American Political Science Association, Washington, D.C., September, 1968.

2. Americans for Democratic Action gave Young and Curtis scores of o for the 1959–60 sessions, and Case a score of 33. See *CQ Weekly Report*, October 7, 1960, p. 1659. On Conservative Coalition votes (votes on which a majority of Northern Democrats opposed a majority of Southern Democrats and a majority of Republicans), Curtis opposed the coalition only 6 per cent of the time; Case, 14 per cent; and Young, 17 per cent. See *CQ Almanac* (1960), pp. 117, 123.

3. I examined the party-support scores and Conservative-Coalition scores supplied by *Congressional Quarterly* for all Republican ranking minority members in the three Congresses for which such scores were available—1959–60, 1963–64, and 1965–66. The mean of all available scores for each congressman was taken. For party support scores see *CQ Weekly Reports*, October 21, 1960, pp. 1723–1727; October 30, 1964, pp. 2590–2592; and December 9, 1966, pp. 2990–2993. A party support vote is defined as a vote on which a majority of the two parties were opposed to each other. Party support for 1961–62 cannot be analyzed since *CQ* used a different measure, which counted only those votes on which a majority of Northern Democrats and a majority of Southern Democrats were in agreement. For *CQ*'s Conservative Coalition scores, see *CQ Almanac* (1960), pp. 117–125; and *CQ Weekly Reports*, November 27, 1964, and December 30, 1966, pp. 3078–3090.

The correlation coefficient between the measure for party support and the measure for "liberalism" in the Senate was $r = -.96$; in the House, $r = -.95$. This finding is supported by Donald R. Matthews, *U.S. Senators and Their World* (New York, Vintage, 1960), p. 134. This inverse relationship, of course, is built into the measures used. But they help describe the ideological cleavage in the Republican party and index a Republican congressman's position in terms of this cleavage.

4. George Goodwin, "The Seniority System in Congress," *American Political Science Review*, June, 1959, pp. 427, 428; Matthews, p. 164. I used *CQ*'s party support scores for all sessions between 1955 and 1966, omitting 1961–62, when a different measure was utilized. *CQ* supplies an "average" party support score for each of the four congressional parties. I calculated the average score of committee leaders in the four groups for each session.

Sources for 1959 on are cited in note 3. For earlier scores, see *CQ Weekly Report*, October 24, 1958, pp. 1343–1347; and ibid., August 31, 1956, pp. 1056–1058.

5. According to *Congressional Quarterly*'s identification and scoring, results are based on Republican support of Eisenhower programs and Democratic support of Kennedy and Johnson programs. See *CQ Weekly Report*, August 10, 1956, pp. 976–987; October 10, 1958, pp. 1267–1279; November 4, 1960, pp. 1803–1814; October 26, 1962, pp. 2038–2046; October 30, 1964, pp. 2595–2597; and December 23, 1966, pp. 3048–3059.

6. For Northern Democrats, 47 per cent of the chairmen had scores between 40 and 59 per cent, compared to only 23 per cent of the members. Only 29 per cent of the chairmen had scores between 60 and 79 per cent, compared to 59 per cent of the members.

7. The same investigation was carried out for levels of party support but provides even less evidence for the influence of congressional seniority. The largest percentage differences between leaders and members occurred in the 80 to 100 and 40 to 59 per cent levels of party support. In the 80 to 100 per cent category were found 17 per cent of scores for committee leaders, 31 per cent for all members, 31 per cent for all members minus first-termers, and 32 per cent for all members elected before 1958. In the 40 to 59 per cent range were found 28 per cent of scores for committee leaders, only 9 per cent for all members, 10 per cent for all members minus first-termers, and 11 per cent for all members elected before 1958. In each case, the per cent for the senior members (those elected before 1958) is closer to the figure for all members than it is to the figure for committee leaders.

8. Western Senators registered a mean score of opposition to the Conservative Coalition of 62 per cent compared to the East's 75 per cent and the Midwest's 73 per cent. Median scores were: West, 61 per cent; East, 75 per cent; and Midwest, 77 per cent.

9. Seventeen of the twenty-six Democratic Senators from the East and Midwest in 1964 were first elected in 1958 or later. The median for years of senatorial service for Senators from both regions was four. Western Senators, by comparison, had spent a median number of eight years in the Senate. Only five of the thirteen Westerners had been first elected from 1958 on.

10. The relationship (or lack of relationship) between years of Senate service and mean per cent score opposed to the Conservative Coalition among Republicans was as follows: more than 20 years, 42 per cent; 15 to 19 years, 12 per cent; 10 to 14 years, 27 per cent; 5 to 9 years, 26 per cent; and 0 to 4 years, 22 per cent. Senator Aiken of Vermont was the one Republican Senator serving more than twenty years.

11. Median scores showed the same general difference; East, 41 per cent; South, 13 per cent; Midwest, 9 per cent; and West, 2 per cent. The

West may well be the most "conservative" region in the Republican party also. The mean score, cited in the text, did not point up this difference because Senator Kuchel's score of 56 per cent raised the average considerably. Of the other seven Westerners, scores ranged between 0 and 11 per cent.

12. George Galloway, *Congress at the Crossroads* (New York, Crowell, 1946), p. 190; see also J. B. Shannon, "Presidential Politics in the South: 1938," Part I, *Journal of Politics*, I (May, 1939), 147. Both writers seem to have the 1932 election in mind. See also Richard Bolling, *House Out of Order* (New York, Dutton, 1965), p. 107.

13. See Frank Freidel, *F. D. R. and the South* (Baton Rouge, Louisiana State University Press, 1965), pp. 1, 30–34; and Arthur M. Schlesinger, Jr., *The Age of Roosevelt: The Crisis of the Old Order*, Vol. I (Boston, Houghton Mifflin, 1957), p. 416.

14. Rexford G. Tugwell, *The Democratic Roosevelt* (New York, Doubleday, 1957), p. 328. See also Freidel, p. 2; and Frances Perkins, *The Roosevelt I Knew* (New York, Viking, 1946), p. 263.

15. Tugwell, pp. 472, 473.

16. James A. Farley, *Jim Farley's Story: The Roosevelt Years* (New York, McGraw-Hill, 1948), pp. 152, 153; Shannon, pp. 147, 148, 283; see also "The GOP Expects," *The Nation*, CIVL (1938), 659, 660.

17. Freidel, pp. 53, 54. See also Harold L. Ickes, *The Secret Diary of Harold L. Ickes: The Inside Struggle, 1936–1939* (New York, Simon and Schuster, 1954), p. 477.

18. For good discussions of the purge attempt, see Shannon, pp. 283ff; and Farley, esp. pp. 121–150.

19. Tugwell, p. 533.

20. Dwight D. Eisenhower, *The White House Years: Mandate for Change, 1953–1956* (New York, Doubleday, 1963), p. 192.

21. Joe Martin, *My First Fifty Years in Politics* (New York, McGraw-Hill, 1960), p. 229.

22. Martin, p. 229. For a good description of the Taft brand of Republicanism, see Clinton Rossiter, *Parties and Politics in America* (Ithaca, N.Y., Cornell University Press, 1960), p. 148. See also Richard H. Rovere, *The Eisenhower Years* (New York, Farrar, Straus and Cudahy, 1956), pp. 103, 104.

23 Eisenhower, pp. 193–195. He lists the Senate "leaders" and then lists the leaders he could "normally count on." Bridges and Millikin, included on the first list, were not included on the second. See also Rovere, p. 103; and Rossiter, p. 147.

24. Robert J. Donovan, *Eisenhower: The Inside Story* (New York, Harper, 1956), p. 37. For other accounts of Eisenhower's troubles with

Congress, see pp. 87–89; and Emmet John Hughes, *The Ordeal of Power* (New York, Atheneum, 1963), p. 144.

25. Eisenhower, p. 202; and Martin, pp. 230, 231.

26. Eisenhower, pp. 218, 303. For a statement of his program, see pp. 285–307; and *CQ Almanac*, pp. 37ff. *CQ* cites Eisenhower, and Eisenhower cites *CQ*!

27. Clinton Rossiter, *The American Presidency*, rev. ed. (New York, Mentor, 1960), p. 52.

6. The Chairmen and Their Committees

1. Nicholas A. Masters, "Committee Assignments in the House of Representatives," in Robert L. Peabody and Nelson W. Polsby, eds., *New Perspectives on the House of Representatives*, 2nd ed. (Chicago, Rand McNally, 1963), p. 244.

2. Ibid., pp. 240, 241.

3. Ibid., pp. 231, 232.

4. William L. Morrow, *Congressional Committees* (New York, Scribner's, 1969), p. 45.

5. Masters, p. 245. For an excellent account of the House Education and Labor Committee, see Richard F. Fenno, Jr. "The House of Representatives and Federal Aid to Education," in Peabody and Polsby, pp. 283–323.

6. Lewis A. Froman, Jr., *The Congressional Process: Strategies, Rubs, and Procedures* (Boston, Little, Brown, 1967), pp. 180, 181.

7. Where a committee was split 50–50, the leverage of the chairman would seem to tip the balance toward similarity rather than dissimilarity. Such cases were therefore included in the Southern-Southern and Northern-Northern categories.

8. See, for example, Stewart L. Udall, "A Defense of the Seniority System," *New York Times Magazine*, January 13, 1957, pp. 17ff.

9. Charles O. Jones, "Joseph G. Cannon and Howard W. Smith: An Essay on the Limits of Leadership in the House of Representatives," *Journal of Politics*, August, 1968, p. 618.

10. John F. Bibby, "The Senate Committee on Banking and Currency," in John F. Bibby and Roger Davidson, *On Capitol Hill* (New York, Holt, Rinehart and Winston, 1967), p. 177.

11. Fenno, p. 299.

12. Ibid.

13. John Bibby and Roger Davidson, "The Senate Committee on Banking and Currency," *On Capitol Hill* (New York, Holt, Rinehart and Winston, 1967), pp. 192–194.

14. Fenno, p. 297.

15. Richard F. Fenno, Jr., "The House Appropriations Committee as a Political System," *American Political Science Review,* June, 1962, pp. 310–324.

16. John F. Manley, "Wilbur P. Mills: A Study in Congressional Influence," *American Political Science Review,* June, 1969, p. 445.

17. Ibid., p. 464.

18. *Final Report of the Joint Committee on the Organization of Congress,* Senate Report 1414, 89th Congress, 2nd Session, 1966, pp. 8–11.

7. Committee Leaders and Party Leaders

1. Richard Bolling, *House Out of Order* (New York, Dutton, 1965), p. 241.

2. Robert L. Peabody, "Party Leadership Change in the House of Representatives," *American Political Science Review,* September, 1967, pp. 675–693.

3. The other three lower in rank held committee positions 4, 6, and 18, respectively. The last was the result of Representative Albert's committee change in the same Congress he became Majority Leader.

4. The distinction between congressmen who have stayed on at least one committee of intial assignment and those who have not may be helpful in distinguishing congressmen who pursue a congressional career through the committee structure and those who pursue it independently of the committee structure. By this measure, career patterns of party and committee leaders differ significantly from one another. Eighty-five per cent of the 127 committee leaders serving from 1957 on had stayed with one committee of initial assignment as opposed to less than half of the party leaders (5 of the 11 or 45 per cent). The average for all senior members was 62 per cent.

5. The recruitment of House leaders is considerably more stable than that in the Senate, especially for the Whip position. The point was illustrated at the beginning of the 91st Congress by the election of Edward Kennedy to the Senate Democratic Whip position over previous incumbent Russell Long, with House Democratic leadership remaining the same. Cf. Randall B. Ripley, *Party Leaders in the House of Representatives* (Washington, D.C., Brookings Institution, 1967), and "The Development of Party Leadership in the United States Senate," unpublished draft.

6. Cf. Peabody's two categories of "revolt" and "challenge to an heir apparent," pp. 484, 485.

7. Peabody.

8. *New York Times*, January 3, 1969.

9. Nelson W. Polsby, "The Institutionalization of the U.S. House of Representatives," *American Political Science Review*, March, 1968, pp. 144–168.

10. I have calculated averages of Polsby's data on per cent of first-term members and mean terms served by incumbents, to parallel the averages Polsby supplies for seniority violations. The correlation coefficient between first-term members and seniority violations is .95, significant at .05; the correlation coefficient between mean terms served by incumbents and seniority violations is −.79, significant at .05.

11. Cf. Richard Fenno, Jr., "The Internal Distribution of Influence: The House," in *The Congress and America's Future*, ed. David B. Truman (Englewood Cliffs, N.J., Prentice-Hall, 1965), the "proportion of new-comers to nonnewcomers is . . . a key index of potential conflict in the House influence structure." See also Charles O. Jones, "The Minority Party and Policy-Making in the House of Representatives," *American Political Science Review*, June, 1968, pp. 482ff; and Peabody, pp. 686–689.

12. *Congressional Quarterly* scores on party support from 1954 to 66 allowed analysis of only eight party leaders. Mean party support scores for 1954–66 are as follows: Senate Democrats, Mansfield 82 per cent, Humphrey 79 per cent, Russell Long 66 per cent; Senate Republicans, Dirksen 78 per cent, Kuchel 59 per cent; House Democrats, Albert 86 per cent, Boggs 83 per cent; and House Republican Ford 76 per cent. For comparison, mean party support scores of all congressional party members, documented in Chapter V, remained stable in the 60–79 per cent range.

13. Boggs registered scores of 79, 81, and 71 per cent in three Congresses before becoming Whip and scores of 93 and 91 per cent afterward.

14. Donald R. Matthews, *U.S. Senators and Their World* (New York, Vintage, 1960), pp. 131, 132. Cf. David B. Truman, ed., *The Congress and America's Future* (Englewood Cliffs, N.J., Prentice-Hall, 1965), pp. 106, 292. Truman comments that the Democrats more than the Republicans managed to fill party leadership positions with moderate, pivotal figures. He is considering Knowland and Wherry as the two Republicans.

15. Peabody, p. 682.

16. See Bolling pp. 207–216; John Bibby and Roger Davidson, "The Senate Committee on Banking and Currency, *On Capitol Hill* (New York, Holt, Rinehart and Winston, 1967), pp. 144–169. Milton C. Cummings, Jr., and Robert L. Peabody, "The Decision to Enlarge the Committee on Rules . . . ," in *New Perspectives on the House of Representatives*, ed. Robert L. Peabody and Nelson W. Polsby, 2nd ed. (Chicago, Rand McNally, 1963), pp. 167–194.

17. Bolling, p. 82.

18. Ibid., p. 216.

19. Joseph Clark, *Congress: The Sapless Branch* (rev. ed., New York, Harper & Row, 1964), p. 132.

20. Ibid., p. 124.

8. The Seniority System and the Congress

1. For interesting comparative data on age and seniority in the United States, German, British, and French parliaments, see Gerhard Loewenberg, *Parliament in the German Political System* (Ithaca, N.Y., Cornell University Press, 1967), pp. 84–90.

2. Roger H. Davidson, David M. Kovenock, and Michael K. O'Leary, *Congress in Crisis: Politics and Congressional Reform* (Belmont, Calif., Wadsworth Publishing Co., 1966), p. 101.

Index

age, of committee chairmen, 20, 96; and seniority rule, 111
Aiken, George, 8
Albert, Carl, 97, 98, 101, 102
Allen, Leo, 79
alphabetical order of names as selection method, 38–39
Anderson, Clinton, 37, 46, 71, 106
apprenticeship process for leaders, 97–100
Arends, Leslie C., 98, 99
assignment to committees. *See* committee assignment

Banking and Currency Committee, 84, 86
Barden, Graham, 90–91, 112
Barkley, Alben, 98, 102, 103
Bible, Alan H., 46
bipartisan nature of congressional committees, 83–84
Boggs, Hale, 98, 101, 104
Bohlen, Charles, 79
Bolling, Richard, 8, 9, 94, 105, 106
bolters from party, seniority loss by, 5–6, 104–5
Bonner, Herbert C., 9

Bricker, John William, 8, 79
Bricker Amendment, 79
Bridges, Styles, 8, 79, 103
Brookhart, Smith, 5
Buckley, Charles, 9
Burleson, Albert S., 9
Butler, Hugh, 79
bypassed congressmen, 28, 32–33
Byrnes, John William, 92

Cannon, Clarence, 8, 10
career patterns of party and committee leaders, 95–100
Case, Francis H., 65
Celler, Emanuel, 3, 9
chairmen of committees. *See* committee chairmen
Chavez, Dennis, 71
Chisholm, Shirley, 85
Clark, Joseph, 11, 38, 90, 105–6
Clay, Henry, 7
Clements, Earle C., 98
Colmer, William, 104–5
committee assignment, changes in, 30–32; and committee seniority, 11; and congressmen's preferences, 85; and geographical rep-